BEING LESBIAN

BEING LESBIAN

LORRAINE TRENCHARD

First published September 1989 by
GMP Publishers Ltd.
PO Box 247, London N17 9QR.

World Copyright © Lorraine Trenchard 1989

Distributed in North America by
Alyson Publications Inc.,
40 Plympton St, Boston, MA 02118, USA

British Library Cataloguing in Publication Data
Trenchard, Lorraine
 Being Lesbian.
 1. Lesbianism
 I. Title
 306.7'663

ISBN 0-85449-113-9

Printed and bound in the EC by Nørhaven A/S, Viborg, Denmark.

For Sharon, with love and thanks
for her love, support and help

Contents

FOREWORD

Don't put this book back on the shelf. If you think you might be a lesbian, or are reading it because you think that someone close to you is a lesbian, then the issues raised in these pages may help prevent a lot of pain and hurt.

Many women who think that they are lesbian, feel very isolated and unsupported. Some try to commit suicide. This book is a reassurance that being lesbian can be a very positive and fulfilling way to lead our lives. Many other women throughout history have lived fruitful lives as lesbians, for instance: [1]

Sappho (c 600 B.C.)	Greek poet
Christine (1626-1689)	Swedish Queen
Gertrude Stein (1874-1946)	Author
Virginia Woolf (1882-1941)	Author
Vita Sackville-West (1892-1962)	Author
Bessie Smith (1894-1937)	Singer
Kate Millet (b 1934,)	Author
Janis Joplin (1943-1970)	Singer

Of course, there are many, many more – some of whom are household names. Lesbians have been around ever since history has been recorded, but attitudes towards us have conspired to make us invisible both in the past and the present.

The lack of positive representation and images isn't only caused by legislation: laws, like prejudice, are created and

1. *The People's Almanac Presents the Book of Lists* Wallenchinsky, Wallace and Wallace, (William Morrow and Company, 1977)

maintained by society. In 1885 the Criminal Law Amendment Act made sex between men illegal, whatever the context. Hearsay has it that lesbians were excluded from this prohibition because Queen Victoria didn't believe that such a thing as love between women could exist.

The word lesbian comes from the followers of the Greek poet Sappho, who lived on the island of Lesbos. It wasn't until 1869 that the word 'homosexual' was coined (homo meaning 'same' rather than 'man' as in 'homo sapien'). It was a hundred years later that lesbians and gay men asserted their collective identity. In 1969 in New York lesbians and gay men stood up against the City Police who were carrying out a routine raid on the Stonewall Inn, a lesbian and gay bar. This incident became known as the Stonewall Riot and is seen as the beginning of the present movement.

Twenty years on from lesbians first standing up and fighting for their rights, we still have a lot of fighting and educating to do. Attitudes are learned and can be challenged and changed. The first step is for us to feel positive about being lesbian.

INTRODUCTION

The importance of words

It is possible to love someone of your own sex, to feel happy about it, and have a lifestyle which reflects that love. Part of the process of getting there is to feel happy about the words which we use to describe ourselves. There are three common ones – homosexual, lesbian and gay. I will be using the word lesbian throughout this book as I consider it the most positive; it reflects the experiences of lesbians, which are often very different to those of gay men. The words *homosexual* and *gay* have become associated in many people's minds only with gay men. The words *lesbian* and *lesbianism* are not open to the same assumption.

Some of the women who have contributed to this book have used the word 'dyke'. Although you might wince at a term which has so often been associated with insults directed at lesbians, it is used in a very positive way by these women. In the same way that black people have reclaimed the word 'black' and now use it as a proud description of themselves, so some lesbians have claimed the word 'dyke' and used it to make the association with strong, independent women. By reclaiming words and making them our own, we are taking the negative connotations out of them. It will then be harder for anyone to use them against us.

It takes some time before we can get used to the sound of certain words which we have previously thought of as pejorative, and think of them as compliments. And despite the children's rhyme about *'sticks and stones may break our bones but words may never hurt us'*, we know that the intention behind words can hurt us very much. The reclaiming of words is one way to reduce the power which they might have to stop us seeing our sexuality in a positive, life-enhancing light.

Women may choose to use different words with different people: parents might react more favourably to the term gay than they would to lesbian, for instance. Some women may change the words they use to describe themselves at different times in their lives. During my first love affair with another woman I thought that I might be bisexual, when my attraction to women continued I thought that I might be homosexual. As I became more confident and comfortable with myself, then *lesbian* became the word I considered most accurately described me.

You might ask why we need words that in some people's opinion label us. The unfortunate fact is that we are already labelled by society – we are presumed to be heterosexual unless we say otherwise. Unless we choose to identify ourselves as women who love women, we will continue to face all the assumptions which go with the label of 'presumed-heterosexual'.

Being happy about being a lesbian is about feeling good about who we are. No one is automatically happy or unhappy because of who they choose to love, but often lesbians are unhappy about their feelings (or, more accurately, made to feel unhappy by other people's reactions and attitudes to their sexuality.) This is one of the issues we will explore in this book.

Who are lesbians? Am I one?

We all grow up in a society that teaches us that homosexuality in general, and lesbianism in particular, is a bad thing. Think about the way school friends talked about lesbians and gay men. Often they hurled words like 'lezzie' and 'poof' at their enemies, thinking that these were the most devastating insults they could inflict. Think about what you've read in newspapers, or heard across the dinner table: if lesbians are mentioned at all it is usually as a threat, a joke or an insult. After years of only hearing detrimental things said about lesbians there's little wonder some women feel badly about their love for other women. We are all subjected to this barrage of negative information, and few of us have the opportunity to hear or see positive things. Is it any wonder then, that the thought of being 'one of those' or 'like that' can be so frightening?

It is not just lesbians who hear all these bad things; everyone gets the same message and unless it's contradicted, there is little reason for them to question what they've been taught. Interestingly, though, once these same people have had the opportunity to meet and talk to positive and open lesbians, they almost always change their attitudes. This also applies to women who have realised that they are lesbian. It happens on two levels: first is the realisation that they are not like the lesbians that others talk about (the myths and stereotypes which we'll examine later). Secondly, when they start to meet other lesbians, they discover that they feel much better about being lesbian themselves.

So, who are lesbians? There isn't one answer to that question. Lesbians come from all groups, backgrounds and ages. You can't tell if a woman is a lesbian just by looking at her – lesbians don't have horns or flashing neon signs. Lesbians are young, old, black, white, married, single, divorced, able-bodied and disabled. They may have children, or have a job, but then again they may not. The only thing that we can definitely say about lesbians is that they are women. They are women who have an emotional and physical attraction to other women.

So how do you know if you are a lesbian? Well, that's for you to decide. Only you will know. Trust your feelings; explore and make sense of your emotions, but don't let anyone else try to tell you how you feel and what you are, whether that is lesbian, bisexual or heterosexual. There are lots of lesbians who have spent years of unhappiness trying to be something they are not. If you think that you might be a lesbian, or are not sure, then hopefully this book will offer some insight into how other lesbians have found their answers. It will offer some advice based on experience. But remember, there are no right answers, no set of rules. Each woman will have to decide what suits her and her situation. What's more, needs may change with time.

The first step is to examine commonly held beliefs about lesbians.

1: EXPLODING THE MYTHS

One of the hardest things about trying to come to terms with our sexuality is finding supportive information. We all grow up in a society where stereotypes of lesbians (the way people think all lesbians look or behave) are very common. Most of these are at best exaggerated generalisations and at worst totally untrue.

Just as generalisations about other minority groups tend to be degrading or dismissive, so too are the ones about lesbians. For example it has been said that lesbians are only 'that way' because they 'can't get a man' or they 'just haven't met the right man yet'. For black lesbians or lesbians with disabilities these stereotypes may be compounded. When we are struggling to create a positive image of ourselves, we need to be reassured that what uninformed people say about lesbians is mostly untrue.

Exploding the myths about lesbians is, therefore, important for us as we take the first step of coming out to ourselves. Then, as confidence grows, and we consider coming out to other people, we will be able to correct any erroneous ideas which they might harbour. It's essential to be ready to answer their questions with conviction. You'll be able to do that if you've thought through the issues before-hand and understand them. Unlike other topics, your friends or family are likely to have been starved of straightforward information about lesbianism, so it's likely they'll depend upon you almost entirely for the facts. Parents particularly will need to be repeatedly reassured that everything is OK.

With this in mind, lets have a look at some of the most common myths. Naturally we can't cover every aspect of the subject, and these are by no means exhaustive explorations of the many misunderstandings that surround us. You should make an effort to read some of the excellent books which lesbians have produced for themselves to grant other perspectives. The more you read, the better you will be able to understand yourself and the reactions of others:

Myth: Lesbians molest children

Statistics show that at least 95 per cent [1] of known child sexual assaults are carried out by heterosexual men (on both girls and boys), often within the family. Lesbians should not be confused with paedophiles (adults who are sexually attracted to young children); most paedophiles define themselves as heterosexual even if they abuse children of the same sex. Again, paedophiles are almost exclusively male.

Myth: Lesbians are only interested in sex

The image of lesbians as rampantly sexual beings with little self-restraint is frankly ludicrous. Certainly lesbians are capable of erotic activity, just like any other woman, but the fact that it doesn't involve men seems to contradict the traditional image of women as passive beings who depend on men for sexual pleasure. Many men find this extremely threatening, hence the idea they have of lesbians being 'different' from other women in their sexual appetites.

Lesbians have as many aspects to their lives as do heterosexual people. Lesbians don't sexually harass straight women, and are far less likely to pursue relationships where the feelings are not returned. Statistics show that the overwhelming incidence of sexual harassment is carried out by heterosexual men against women.

1. For example; *Child Sexual Abuse: New Theory and Research* by David Finklehor (Free Press, 1984)
Father-daughter sexual abuse: the abuse of Paternal Authority by Angie Ash (Social Theory and Institutions Publications, 1984)

Myth: Lesbians don't have children

Many lesbians do have children. Being lesbian doesn't mean you are infertile. Some lesbian women have children from earlier relationships with men; some choose to have children by A.I.D. (Artificial Insemination by Donor.) Recently local authorities have encouraged lesbians to become foster parents, and some have done so successfully. Adopting children, however, is a much more complicated business since the legal system tends to discriminate against lesbians. This legal discrimination is also apparent when lesbians are involved in child custody disputes which need to be resolved in court.

Myth: Lesbians have unstable relationships

Unstable compared to what? One in four marriages ends in divorce; one in seven families in Britain are single parent. These statistics hardly seem to indicate that heterosexuals have found a magic formula for making relationships work. And yet the establishment clings to the idea that 'Christian marriage' between men and women is the only acceptable way to live.

Studies have shown that lesbians are similar to heterosexual women in terms of the length of relationships they have. But there is a difference: there are no marriage contracts for lesbian couples, no pressure to stay together from family or friends, and no need to 'keep up appearances'. If they are together, you can be sure it's because they want to be.

Myths about how we look

There are many myths about how lesbians look: they always wear men's clothing (particularly dungarees), never wear dresses, have short cropped hair and are ugly. The truth is that lesbians are as diverse as the general population. You can't tell by just looking at a woman whether or not she is a lesbian. Women who don't fit the stereotypes are presumed not to be lesbian, and those who do are. In most cases, both counts are wrong.

Myths about why we are lesbian

These are numerous, and often contradictory. The theories vary from the pseudo- medical (hormone imbalance, genetics, mental illness), to pseudo-psychological, (dominant mother, dominant father, no brothers, no sisters, faulty emotional development.) Other theories blame bad experiences with men (or even no experience with men.) Then there is the seduction theory: women are 'converted' to lesbianism by an older woman.

There have been many attempts over the past century to prove one or other of these theories, and none has convincingly succeeded. So what are we left with? Some women are lesbian, some are heterosexual – and that is as much as can be categorically stated. You will notice that no one ever asks what causes people to be heterosexual.

Myth: Lesbians try to convert or influence others

This common myth is often used to try and prevent lesbians coming into contact with young 'impressionable' girls. Obstacles are frequently put in the way of lesbian women becoming teachers, mothers or youth workers. It is also cited as an argument against having positive images of lesbians in libraries, in films and on TV.

But if it were so easy to persuade someone to change their sexuality, why aren't we all heterosexual? After all, from the moment we are born we are flooded with images and information about heterosexuality. We are told that being straight is the only true way, and that homosexuality is bad, funny or tragic. In the face of all this, why do some of us still turn out to be lesbian?

Sexuality is not as fragile and malleable as some claim. What can and does happen is that meeting other lesbians, or seeing positive information gives courage to women who think that they may be lesbians to feel good about who they are.

Myth: Lesbians are women who want to be men

This confuses lesbians with transexuals. Women who want to have a sex change and become men are less common than men who want to be women. Transexuals nearly always define themselves as heterosexual. It must be said however, that there are some women who feel attracted to other women, but who have no support or information to translate what they feel into terms they can understand. They think they would like to be men because they would then be able to have relationships with women in a way that is comprehensible to them. Most lesbians are very happy being women, and celebrate their gender.

Myth: Lesbians are all white

This is part of the myth that lesbians are all the same. We're not, and I say again: lesbians are as diverse as women in general. Many lesbians are black or from other ethnic minorities, they are old as well as young, some are women with disabilities and some are working class. It is often easier for white, middle-class, able-bodied women with no children to be open about being lesbian. Those who face other discrimination take more risks by coming out: lesbians with disabilities may lose the support they need to survive; black lesbians may lose the support they need in a racist society; lesbian mothers may lose custody of their children.

There is not one lesbian community, but many. Some women who face additional discrimination sometimes choose to organise in autonomous groups where they will get support from women who share their experience. Black lesbians, or lesbians from other ethnic minorities, who face racism in a predominantly white society (from other lesbians as well as generally) may gain strength from being together. There are also groups organised on the basis of a shared culture, whether that is Jewish, Irish, Muslim, Latin American or whatever. Lesbian mothers, and lesbians with disabilities have also formed groups (see resources list.)

Myth: Lesbians are at risk from AIDS and HIV

Lesbians are one of the groups least at risk from AIDS or HIV (or any other sexually transmitted disease.) However, should lesbians also inject drugs and share their injecting equipment, they may be vulnerable to infection with HIV or Hepatitis B. Heterosexual women are more likely to get infected with HIV from sexual activity than are sexually active lesbians. More about this in the chapter on health.

These are some of the most common myths and stereotypes, and hopefully some facts to help counter them. You are almost bound to come across people who will react badly to your lesbianism on what can generally be called religious or moral grounds. Let's take a look at some possible responses to those arguments:

"It's not natural, it's against nature"

Natural implies things that happen in nature. Homosexuality has been around for as long as history has been recorded, in all cultures. It has also been documented as occurring in other animal species.

What most people mean when they come up with the 'unnatural' argument is that lesbian sex is non-procreative (children can't be conceived) and that therefore it's a threat to the survival of the species. Two issues arise from this. One is the existing size of the earth's population: many would maintain that there are already too many people using up diminishing resources, do we really need more? The second is that there are a substantial number of heterosexual couples who cannot – or choose not to – have children. Are these relationships 'unnatural' by the same token?

In this day and age, with easily obtained contraception and increased sexual freedom, few sexual encounters – even within marriage – are solely for the sake of conception. Other sexual practices, like masturbation, are quite clearly not aimed at procreation. In addition, remember that many lesbians can, and do, have children.

"It's against my religion"

This is more problematic since people who say it usually hold very strong views and often don't want them challenged. After all, love, happiness and respect are the cornerstones of most religions – although it is sometimes difficult to remember this when religiously-motivated individuals pour scorn and hatred upon us.

A more pragmatic line of argument is that, in terms of Christianity, the Bible contains many laws and prohibitions which are either impractical to follow, or are unacceptable in today's world. Whilst slavery, crucifixions and stoning were accepted without question in Biblical times they would be regarded as repellent to modern social attitudes. Dietary, sanitary and other laws of behaviour, suited to earlier times, would no longer be practical. People highlight those parts of the Bible which reflect their own attitudes, and ignore those parts which don't. In South Africa, for example, the Government uses Christianity and the Bible to justify apartheid. How many of the people who quote Sodom and Gommorah actually pay one tenth of their wages to the church each

21

month, as stipulated in the Bible? There is argument, anyway, about what exactly the Bible story of Sodom and Gommorah really means. Some scholars insist that it is more to do with a breach of the laws of hospitality than about homosexuality.

Remember that Jesus never said a word about homosexuality, if however you have strong religious feelings, which you see as conflicting with your sexuality, seek out other lesbians who hold similar beliefs, for example the Catholic Lesbian Sisterhood or the Lesbian and Gay Christian Movement. They will be able to show you an alternative way to reconcile your sexuality with your religious convictions. If religion is going to be an issue with family or friends, it may be useful to get in contact with one of the groups listed in the back of this book, and to read some of the literature which has been written on the subject.

2: COMING OUT

Coming out is a term which lesbians use when they tell someone about their sexuality. However, coming out usually begins on a much more personal level – acknowledging to ourselves that we are lesbian. Deciding that we are lesbian can be a long and tortuous business, often involving denials, evasions and self-delusion. However, when we've got it sorted out in our minds, we can begin to make rapid progress towards a more fulfilled life as a lesbian. Although it's only the initial stage, it's a pretty important one. The need for self-acknowledgement is one of the things which make lesbians different from other oppressed groups:

> We first become identified as part of the gay minority by ourselves rather than by others, and thus as an isolated individual.[1]

Coming out is not an easy thing for most lesbians, partly because it is such a personal decision and needs much strength, and partly because it is something which we have to do alone. By accepting yourself as a lesbian you are issuing yourself with a number of daunting challenges. By keeping quiet you can avoid these difficult issues, but by the same token you will be cutting yourself off from the possibility of making a life that fully satisfies you.

Coming out as lesbian is different, for instance, from being black. If you are black then other people will identify you as belonging to a minority group, and they may treat you differently or discriminate against you because of your

1. *Sexuality* by Jeffrey Weeks (Tavistock Publications Limited, 1986)

colour. If you are a lesbian it is you who must acknowledge that you belong to a minority group in this society. If you are black you can readily see who else belongs to your group; you will have parents who are black, black friends, black teachers, you may have favourite movie stars or sports stars who are black. There are people around who serve as role models, who can share with you their experience of what it is like to be black – in both positive and negative terms.

If you are a lesbian then your experience will be quite different; it is likely that you will have heterosexual parents, friends and role models. You will have been brought up observing/sharing their experience of heterosexuality – again both the positive and negative aspects. Unless you were very lucky, it is unlikely that you will have been able to share your feelings about your sexuality with them. As a lesbian (unlike some other minority groups), you cannot count upon secure support from your family. Anti-lesbian feelings within the home as well as outside it mean that lesbians have a double burden. Therefore, finding other lesbians to talk through your experiences is one of the most important and positive steps you can take. Before that, however, you have to be honest with yourself.

Coming out, finding out

You can't demand as a right that other people treat you with dignity; they will only accord you such respect if they perceive that you value yourself sufficiently to be taken seriously. Your own self-esteem (or lack of it) will signal to others how they should react to you. If you are humble and apologetic people will bully and manipulate you. If you are honest, open and confident others will react to you with appropriate regard.

It has been said that you can't really love someone else until you love yourself. If you've acknowledged to yourself that you are a lesbian and are still living and behaving in ways that are dictated by others you may be missing out on relationships and experiences not because you want to, but because you've allowed other people to make the decision for you. If you don't respect your needs and feelings, you may be risking your happiness and eroding your self-esteem.

Sometimes it may be a while before you can actually take any action, for example:

> I was married, had two kids, a mortgage and the whole bit, but   there was something missing. I began to wonder if I was a lesbian even before I got married, I always had fantasies about being with women, even when I was in bed with my husband. I waited till the kids left home before I did anything about it. I feel like I wasted a lot of my life, but the children were important.

Or

> My folks would have gone crazy. They were very religious. I left home as soon as I could and then came out.

Letting other people determine how we should lead our lives undermines our right to make decisions about ourselves. It's essential that we take control of our destiny and demand that our decisions are respected. Putting other people's opinions about us above our own is generally self-defeating. It usually means that no one ends up fulfilled or happy, and it may create a lot of resentment and frustration.

There is, of course, another route to realising that you are a lesbian: falling in love with a woman and possibly having a relationship. Often everything seems right and good and it is only when others make comments or give your feelings a name that you realise that you are a lesbian:

> I hadn't considered the possibility of loving women, then zap! I was in love. All of a sudden the soppy love songs about which I had always been so cynical made sense. I didn't think that I was a lesbian, I just thought that I had fallen in love, and

the object of that love just happened to be another woman.

There is no one age or set of experiences which determines when coming out is right. Women might come to terms with their sexuality when they are fifteen or fifty, when they are living at home or after leaving, before having relationships with men or after being married for years. I could fill a book with coming out stories, every one different from the other. Each woman is unique, and each will have a different set of experiences and so we can only generalise when discussing the known facts about lesbianism; the emotions won't fit into neat pigeon holes.

One of the most frequently asked questions is: 'How do you know that you are a lesbian if you've never slept with women?' This brings us back to you – only you can say how you feel and what is going on in your head. You are the sole expert on you, don't ever give the job to anyone else. People never ask how teenage heterosexuals know that they are heterosexual – even when they haven't had a sexual relationship with the opposite sex.

There is another side to this question; some women ask, 'I slept with a woman, does that mean I'm a lesbian?' The answer to this may sometimes be 'no', but the experience is nonetheless a healthy way of exploring alternative options. Sometimes the answer is 'yes', but that answer is not because of the sexual act but because of the emotions involved and brought to the surface. Identifying yourself as a lesbian is, in fact, less about sexual activity than about how you feel, your emotions or who you fantasize about.

Coming out positively

Many lesbians report that although they realised they were attracted to other women, they imagined that they were the only one in the world who felt that way. This sense of total isolation can be one of the most frightening periods on the way to becoming happy with your sexuality. Rose Robertson of *Parents Enquiry*, a counselling organisation for the parents of lesbians and gay men, says that in her experience the majority of young people spend an average of two years in emotional isolation, unable to talk to anyone about their sexual feelings.

However, after acknowledging their sexuality to themselves, most lesbians will eventually – maybe after months or even years – want to share the knowledge with someone else. (For some individuals – for example lesbian nuns – this is as far as it goes. Although they may acknowledge their sexuality and maybe even share the knowledge with others, they keep their vows of celibacy.) [2]

There is no doubt that re-evaluation and change can be painful. In coming to terms with our sexuality we have to start resisting all those myths and stereotypes which have been foisted on us over the years. We have to question other people's values, and start questioning our own ideas. The emotional roller-coaster ride which goes with sorting out our sexuality can be made more bearable by speaking to women who are sure about their lesbianism. But if you are isolated and don't know any 'out' lesbians, how do you find someone to talk things over with?

For a lot of women, the lesbian telephone lines which operate all over the country are an unthreatening, anonymous and reassuring source of information. Lesbian lines are staffed by lesbians who are more than happy to talk through their experiences, and to listen to what you may be going through. Many of the women who join lesbian lines do so because they themselves phoned a line when they were first coming out and found it very helpful. Lesbian liners do not see themselves as experts, merely women who have gone through the coming out process and are willing to help others to do the same where possible. Because the volunteers are 'ordinary women', you may also find that they may have been in similar situations to yourself (at school, in marriage, living in a small village etc.) or may have had similar experiences (crushes on friends or colleagues, unfulfilling

2. *Breaking the Silence: Lesbian Nuns on Convent Sexuality* Eds. Rosemary Curb and Nancy Manahan (Columbus Books, 1985)

relationships with men.) There are usually a number of volunteers working on any Lesbian Line or Gay Switchboard, so you can call up and talk to different women and share their varied experiences.

Dialling a complete stranger and talking to her about something you've never articulated before can be a frightening prospect, but remember that Lesbian Line volunteers all had to take this difficult initial step themselves at some stage:

> I can't remember where I got the number from, but I do remember that the first time I phoned I simply couldn't talk. I just listened to a very normal-sounding voice on the other end, trying to get some response. That happened a few times. Then I talked and talked. Now, when I'm working on the Line and we get these 'silent calls', I recall my own experience and sympathise.

Gay Switchboards may also be established in your area. They may have women working on them, or you could talk to a gay man. Find out which service is closest to you, it saves on telephone bills. You'll be surprised just how much you have to say once you get started.

To find out the number of your nearest Lesbian Line or Gay Switchboard try:

★ Looking it up in the telephone directory, yellow pages or local directory.

★ Telephoning one of the Lesbian Lines or Gay Switchboards listed in the back of this book.

★ Looking for listings in magazines, especially those which have a lesbian and gay section or which are specifically for lesbians and/or gay men.

★ Enquire at your local reference library.

Another useful and safe way to begin exploring sexuality is by reading. There are a number of books available which deal with the lives and experiences of lesbians in just about every type of circumstance. There are romances, historical novels, detective stories, humour and science fiction books. The only advice I have is to steer clear of any psychology books (usually written by men) where homosexuality is dealt with as a sexual deviation or clinical problem.

Finding positive books is not difficult – you found this one, after all! Libraries are the cheapest way to get hold of books, and it might help to look for titles which are published by the feminist or gay publishing houses like Virago, Sheba, The Women's Press, Pandora and GMP. Each volume usually lists other books from the same publisher, which will help you find further reading material. Some forward-looking local authorities have actually produced lists of books of specific interest to lesbians – all of them available on their shelves.

If you can afford to buy books 'alternative', women's, gay and, increasingly, the general bookshops are all sources of relevant reading. They will also be able to tell you what is newly available, or give you advice about books you are seeking. As an alternative to personal shopping (which can be an ordeal for someone still struggling with their sexuality) you can use the mail order facilities offered by some bookshops (see listings.) A number of books are available on audio tape for those with reading difficulties.

Likewise, lesbian and gay newspapers and magazines are a useful source of information, not just to find out the number of local telephone help lines, but as a means of locating clubs, pubs and youth groups. They also provide news and discussions about subjects of interest to lesbians and gay men – all seen from a refreshingly positive point of view.

Recently there have been a number of films which deal with lesbian relationships in a positive way (*Desert Hearts, The Colour Purple, I've Heard the Mermaids Singing*). You might find it interesting to see these either at the cinema, or on video. It's quite a thrill, after a lifetime of having to watch films about heterosexual relationships, suddenly to see films which echo our own feelings and experiences.

The first steps

★ Trust your feelings – and stop letting other people dictate your lifestyle.

★ Telephone a lesbian line – it could be the first step to a whole new life.

★ Raid your local library or bookshop – and if they don't have the titles you want, order them.

★ Go to the cinema to see a genuine portrayal of lesbian experience in films made by lesbians. And if you missed them on the big screen, catch the video.

★ Find other lesbians to talk to – it's amazing what an effect shared experiences can have on confidence.

Coming out is a continuing process. Each time we meet someone or start a new job, we have to decide whether we should tell them about our sexuality. Many lesbians resist coming out because they say they don't need to 'shout it from the rooftops'. But there is no need to make a general announcement to the whole world in order to share this important aspect of yourself with the people you love and care about.

Each time the issue of coming out arises you will have to assess the merits of taking the plunge, taking into account your unique set of circumstances. Only you can decide whether it is wise or appropriate to come out at any given moment.

If you have acknowledged to yourself that you are a lesbian, you've taken the hardest step of all. From here on you'll gain strength and determination from the experience.

And by effectively placing yourself in a minority group you will be better placed to sympathise with the discrimination faced by other groups in society. You will, hopefully, understand the frustration and powerlessness faced by our black sisters or women with disabilities. If we expect others to challenge the discrimination against lesbians, then we must acknowledge and counter our own prejudices.

3: COMING OUT TO FAMILY AND FRIENDS

The word 'family' has a lot of different meanings in our society. For those brought up in care, it might mean people who had an important role in their early lives. For older or married women, it may mean children, grandchildren or husband. Not all of those who were brought up within 'families' are still in touch with their parent/s.

The home situation will be different for all kinds of people: young women might live with their parent/s, whilst a married woman might share her home with a husband and children of her own. It follows that there is no set answer to the question: should I come out to my family? If your answer is yes, there then follows the dilemma about the best way to come out to the sort of 'family' you might be part of. As in earlier chapters, we can look at the experience of others and try to learn from them.

Why come out to families?

★ It allows you to be honest about who you are and what you are doing in your life.

★ It takes away the stress of having to lead a 'double life', of watching your every word in case you let the cat out of the bag.

★ It means that you no longer have to worry about either being 'found out', or having an outsider break the news to your family.

★ It means that you can share the good times, and the bad times in all parts of your life with someone who loves you.

In general, those who have come out to their families find the ensuing honesty and openness a great relief. Having said that, some have found initial difficulties – first reactions were negative, but improved over time and with education.

Young lesbians

Being young means that you lack power, and are often dependent upon other people (parents usually) to support you. Adults – whether parents or guardians – have rights and powers under the law which they can exert over you. This is especially true if you are under 16.

Although lesbian mothers and gay fathers aren't unknown of course, your parents will very probably be heterosexual. Most of the extended family – grandparents, uncles, aunts, cousins etc – will also be heterosexual. There is usually an assumption among them that you, too, are heterosexual. As far as most families are concerned lesbians are someone else's children. It follows that one of the main problems in coming out to parents is that they hardly ever consider the possibility that their offspring might be lesbian or gay. They never have to question or challenge the myths and stereotypes because the topic is about 'someone else', not their own little darling whom they love and who seems very 'normal'. Their shock, horror or disbelief when the bombshell drops, therefore, may be extreme. Then again, it is always possible that they might turn the tables and surprise you by being supportive and accepting from the start. Some women have been pleasantly surprised:

> I was really scared that my dad would do the whole 'don't darken my doorway again' routine. That's one of the reasons why I waited until I had a network of supportive friends before I broached the subject. We were walking downstairs and I

said 'I want to tell you something', and when he said 'What?', I said 'I think I'm gay, and he just said 'okay'. He was fine. I said 'We're meant to have a big row,' and he said, 'The dinner's getting cold, I'll think about it while we eat'. Then he said that it was okay by him and he really couldn't be bothered to have an argument if that was alright with me.

There is no rule that says you must come out to your parents. Nor is there a formula for telling you when, where or how. For some women there are special factors which have to be taken into account. If the family's reaction to their lesbianism is bad, black and other minority ethnic lesbians risk losing the support they get from their families in the face of racism. Women with disabilities might be physically dependent upon other people to survive; the risks they take in coming out may be greater than those taken by a white woman who is economically and socially independent.

Others who are distant from their families, either emotionally or geographically, may not feel that the question of coming out is pressing. In all cases, you are the final judge as to whether you want to come out or not.

Telling parents

Below are examples of how some lesbians have reported their parents' reactions when they first came out as lesbian (in italic) and how they feel now. These quotes are from women under 21 years old living in London: [1]

> *Wonderfully, but slightly concerned about my happiness, believed in some of the myths about lesbians until I talked a lot with her about it...*
> She totally accepts it and respects my decision.
> (Age 17)

1.*Talking about Young Lesbians* by Lorraine Trenchard, London Gay Teenage Group (1984)

Very upset – tried to finish the relationship by a court injunction. I became very distant from them...
Fine – let me live as I want to, try to understand me as best they can. Accept the situation and take an interest in my romances, proud to take me and my girlfriend out socially.(Age 2O)

My mother got drunk, tried to beat me up and my father asked me to leave...
Fine. They want to be part of my life, they love my girlfriend and they understand. (Age 2O)

Really understanding. My Mum is brill.
Really happy, I go and visit her with my lover, and always have with lovers. (Age 17)

As you can see from the above examples, the initial reaction of parent/s is often negative, but over a period of time these usually change to acceptance, and often positive support. If you do choose to tell your parents, a little forward planning can help you create the best circumstances for a favourable response.

★ They will probably expect you to bring the subject up. Do this when relations between you are good – don't throw it at them in the middle of an argument.

★ Be prepared to answer questions and deal with myths.

★ Be positive about yourself and who you are.

★ The more you sound like you are sharing something important with them, and the less like an aggressive announcement, the more likely they are to listen rather than be defensive.

★ It might be worth having some books or leaflets on hand for them to read and digest.

★ Even if you plan to come out to parents who are geographically distant, for example by writing a letter, think about these points, try to anticipate their questions and answer them truthfully.

One of the most important steps is to think the issues through. Make sure you understand what is involved before you try to explain it to them. You may find it helpful to speak to someone on one of the Lesbian Lines or Gay Switchboards. Try 'testing the water' by bringing up the subject with them in an abstract way and gauging their response. But remember, they might react differently if they think they are talking about a stranger 'out there' than if they are talking about someone whom they love.

Reactions

Thousands of lesbians and gay men have come out to their parents, and so many thousands of parents have had to deal with the news that their child is lesbian or gay. Even so, the way they respond and the questions they ask remain fairly predictable.

Where did I/we go wrong?

This response is based on the fact that many parents see being lesbian as negative. They think that you are suffering because of some emotional or physiological deficiency for which they are responsible. The best way to counter this is to emphasise that you are happy being the way you are, that it is nobody's 'fault'. If anything, you want to thank them for allowing you the space and giving you the support to make decisions for yourself – even if they are contrary to expectations.

It's just a phase

This reassurance is given to young people who may have experimented with different relationships but then decide that they are heterosexual. It helps alleviate parents' feelings of guilt, but creates problems for people who go on to decide that they ARE lesbian (or gay.) The best answer is that for some people it might be true, but for many others – yourself included – it is much more than that. Point out that if homosexuality were just a phase that young people passed through there wouldn't be groups for older lesbians and gay men and nor would there be lesbian and gay couples who had life long relationships. If you can convince them that you have thought about it long and hard and that it isn't a 'fad', they may listen to you more seriously.

You have been influenced/converted.
This is another common reaction – it deflects responsibility from them or you to a third party. The first point to make here is that you are old enough and sensible enough to make decisions about yourself and your life. It might be worth giving them an example of another big decision you made and with which they agreed, for example staying on at school, leaving home, breaking up with a boyfriend in the past. You then have to work through the myth about lesbians converting other (especially younger) women. Have a read through the section on exploding the myths before you tell them.

There is something wrong with you, you should see a psychiatrist.
This reaction reflects all the myths about illnesses and psychological problems. The important point to make is that you are not sick or unbalanced. Do not let them send you to your local GP, or to a psychiatrist. Although some medical people are OK, many have very strange ideas about lesbianism. Even with the best motivation in the world, if a doctor starts from the premise that lesbianism is unhealthy, he or she is likely to end up doing more harm than good.

It might be worth pointing out to your parents that hiding your lesbianism from them has been very stressful. Go on to say that now you are sure, the one thing that would make your life easier would be for them to accept. Point out to them the anxiety involved in concealing the truth is far more hazardous to your health than your lesbianism.

Being dragged out

If someone else tells your parents, or if they find out some other way (by reading your mail for example), then they may raise the subject first. The disadvantage of this is that you will be caught off guard. Don't panic. Try to turn this into something positive (remember that they have saved you the trouble of having to bring up the subject.) Parents who have found out from some third party may have spent some time agonising over the information. Try to take control of the situation. There is not much point in denying the fact, especially if you had planned to come out anyway. It will only create more tension if they are suspicious and negative. Reassure them, work through the myths and try to stay calm and dignified.

Crisis intervention

If things go really badly, whether it is you or someone else who brings up the topic, then think about getting help from other people. You need support for yourself. Sometimes just talking through what has happened with other lesbians will make you feel better. Being reassured that other people have been there and survived can be a great comfort. A Lesbian Line or lesbian group/friends will be useful at this point.

There are groups and telephone lines set up for parents of lesbians and gay men, it might be worth giving them a ring for advice about the next step. Another alternative is to get a third person in to try and mediate and reassure your parents. An older person whom they respect is the ideal. But make sure they know what they're talking about and that they're really on your side.

If you have told other members of your family – brothers, sisters, aunts, uncles, grandparents – and had a good response, bring them in as allies. They could help in getting your parents to calm down and listen. Finally, if you think that they are beyond reason, put things on ice for a while.

Remember, parents often react very badly at the beginning, but change their attitudes when they've had time to let it sink in. Meanwhile, conduct yourself with dignity and give them space to do their thinking.

Don't avoid mentioning your sexuality again, but do plan a more structured and creative discussion with them as soon as they are ready.

There is of course the possibility that your parent/s may not be able to cope with the fact that their daughter is a lesbian, and refuse totally to discuss the subject. Many young lesbians have been thrown out of home when their parent/s have found out. This happened to one in ten of the young lesbians who were surveyed by the *London Gay Teenage Group Research* project (1984.)[2]

If this happens, you may have to strike out on your own. Remember that it is them, not you, who has decided to make your coming out into a big problem. They can choose to react more calmly and then any distress can be minimised. Seek out advice and support from other lesbians.

Many lesbians take the decision to move away from their family circles and set up home with other lesbians as a support network, a kind of alternative family. It may be that your parents will eventually come to accept the fact that you are a lesbian, but instead of being in their control and at their mercy, your independence from them will allow you to meet them on your own terms. There are special housing projects for young people who are thrown out of their family home. If you are homeless because of your sexuality, ring Lesbian and Gay Switchboard in London and ask for advice.

Parents have to come out too

We often forget that parents have to 'come out' as well. They have to 'come out' as having a lesbian daughter. They have to face the questions of their neighbours, friends and relatives

2. *Something to tell you* by Lorraine Trenchard and Hugh Warren, London Gay Teenage Group (1984)

about what you are up to, who you are going out with – and when you are getting married. The better they feel about you being a lesbian, the sooner they will stop saying you are a 'career girl' or avoiding the questions in some other way.

Make it clear that you feel happy and positive about yourself, and encourage your parents to talk honestly about you to their friends. Tell them that you know what it's like being unable to talk to anyone about lesbianism. Acknowledge that they will have to 'come out' and help them through the process as best you can – including dealing with the myths and stereotypes. You could touch on this when you have the 'coming out' discussion with them.

Having raised the subject, one of the problems lots of lesbians face is how to bring it up again, especially if parents are avoiding discussing it. Talking to them about how they feel about their own need to come out may be a useful tactic – it focuses the attention on them and identifies their worries.

Other members of the family

Coming out to other members of the family sometimes happens before telling parents and sometimes after. Much will depend on who you feel close to. If you feel closer to siblings fine, but you might feel more comfortable with an older relative who is slightly removed.

Just as some young lesbians have a lesbian mother, other women have gay brothers, lesbian sisters, aunts, cousins and so on. If someone has come out in your family, especially your close family, then their trail blazing may be invaluable.

Having a whole family who knows and accepts that you are lesbian can be a wonderful support. It means that family occasions, like Christmas dinner, weddings and so on become events where you are invited to bring your partner. If there is a death in the family, then being out means that your family acknowledge that you may want support from your partner, just as heterosexual brothers and sisters may want their partners there.

Coming out – what about my children?

Some women may have left home and had a relationship with a man, perhaps getting married, perhaps having their own children. Some women think that their feelings are just 'a phase' and that marriage will 'cure them'. For these and other women who come out when they are older, there may be different considerations.

If you are married and have children when you acknowledge that you are lesbian then the main thing to remember is this: if you want custody of the children don't tell your husband that you are a lesbian. Even if you think that he will understand and be supportive, you might find a contested custody case will bring out the worst in a father who is threatened. You have to accept that the courts still don't usually give lesbian mothers custody of their children. Make a break, sort out the custody and then, when all is secure, you will have the freedom to decide without putting your choices in jeopardy. There are organisations and books which can give you more advice. See the resources list.

If your husband does know that you are a lesbian, there are various things which may help you win custody of the children whether you are separated or not.

★ Keep the children with you whether you move out or not.

★ Keep a note of violence, threats or missed visits. Write them down with a note of the date and circumstances.

★ Get in touch with a lesbian mothers group, not just for support, but also for advice.

★ Get in touch with the Lesbian Custody Project for specialist information. They also have lists of supportive solicitors.

Coming out to your children

How you approach this will be dependent upon how old they are. If they are grown up then the issue usually revolves around convincing them that you have a right to relationships with whoever you choose. Many offspring forget that their mothers have sexual and emotional needs, and that her life might consist of more than simply playing the role of mother to them.

Younger children raise different issues. The first point to make is that the children of lesbians are usually well-adjusted, sensitive and totally unperturbed by their mother's sexuality. [3] What is important for any child is the quality and quantity of love and care they receive. It seems irrelevant whether this comes from one or two women (or from a heterosexual couple.) If you want to be honest with your children and live your life openly, then the issue needs to be addressed. Just as with coming out to parents, it is better if you can initiate discussion rather than waiting to respond to accusations or questions.

Some guidelines:

★ Take the initiative.

★ You feel positive about being lesbian, make sure this gets over to your children. A long face and 'heavy' atmosphere will set the wrong tone.

★ Don't expect them to guess what you are trying to say – 'I expect you know what I am going to tell you, don't you?'

★ Anticipating your children's questions might make answering them easier, for example: 'Will I be a lesbian, too?' or 'Can I tell my friends?'

3. Studies have been done which indicate that the children of lesbians do not have any more problems than children from single parent households, or heterosexual families. For example;

42

★ Even if they have heard about lesbians, it is important that you explain what being lesbian means to you. Like the rest of us, what they've heard is probably negative and derogatory.

★ Don't ignore the issue once you have told them. Like coming out to other members of your family, it's useful to include the subject in all manner of everyday conversations.

Coming out to friends

Your first coming out might be to a friend. It could be someone at school, a work colleague or a neighbour. It might be a man or a woman who, in turn, might be straight or lesbian/gay. If the friend is important to you, you will probably want to be be honest about your sexuality; as with members of the family, it's difficult to have a proper relationship with friends when you can't be open. If friends feel that you are holding back on them, they may hold back on you, and the resulting distance can lead to the friendship fizzling out. Some friends are particularly hurt if they feel they haven't been trusted with the confidence earlier. Many women discover that, despite their fears and reservations, their friends already know the truth or had suspected it.

In fact, telling friends can be a bit of an anti-climax; you spend weeks planning your coming out speech, perhaps even arranging a special meal or outing. Then towards the end of the evening, having repeatedly put it off, you grimly announce that you have Something to Say. Your friend expects the worst – is it drugs or a criminal conviction, perhaps? When you eventually manage to spit it out, all they can say is 'Oh, is that all? Yes, I guessed'.

Even so, be prepared to talk through all the issues with them, and to answer all manner of questions. By the time you get to sleep in the early hours of the morning the only thing you're likely to regret is that you didn't do it all earlier.

Friends worth having will either already have a pretty good idea, or will want to understand and support you. This doesn't mean, however, that everyone you think of as a friend will react this way. There are two extreme possibilities:

The positive: 'Yes, I am too'. It's surprising how often this happens. When you're so caught up in being defensive, it's easy to miss similar behaviour in other people. Each time they raise the issue to test the water you presume that they are trying to get you to say something 'incriminating' about your own sexuality. If you are being very defensive you might say something negative about lesbianism to put them off the trail, and they in turn give up trying to get the topic talked about.

The negative: Some people might change their opinion of you and not want to know you any more after they discover that you are a lesbian. Although it's not always easy, try to identify these people before you come out to them. Many of those who react in a negative way initially will, after some reflection, change their attitude. Those who don't (and don't want to) accept the news can be dangerous: they may feel obliged to come out for you to other friends, family and perhaps work colleagues. Remember, if you do find yourself in this situation, the best way to minimise the damage is to feel positive about yourself. People who try to use your lesbianism against you in some spiteful way usually end up showing themselves in a bad light. Their own vindictiveness will count against them in other people's estimation. They are the sort of people you don't need as friends.

Always bear in mind in such situations: it is not you who has the problem, it is the so-called friend who is suffering from homophobia (as the fear of homosexuals and homosexuality has been called.)

★ Friends worth having are friends who like you for what and who you are.

★ Friendships worth keeping are based on honesty and trust – from both sides.

★ Friends often already have an idea that you are lesbian and are just waiting for you to 'give them permission' to discuss it.

★ Those who don't initially accept may need time to come round to the idea – give them space and time to think it through.

★ Try and identify those who may not be able to accept your lesbianism before you come out to them. You can do this by discussing the topic generally and gauging their reactions.

Children in Lesbian and Single Parent Households by Susan Gollombok, Ann Spencer, Michael Rutter, (Institute of Psychiatry, 1983. Vol 24 no 4. p551-572)

Lesbian Mothers and their children, a comparative survey, M. Kirkpatrick, M. Smith, R. Roy (American Journal of Orthopsychiatry, 1981. Vol 5. no 13. pp54 5-551)

4: COMING OUT AT WORK

As we've seen, coming out is an unending process, and not something to which general rules can be applied. Every time you meet new friends, start a new job or find you have a new colleague you will have to decide whether or not to come out to them. Just as you may not choose to tell everyone who frequents the local pub that you are a lesbian, you may choose to tell everyone (or no-one) at work.

However, like the other decisions which you make about coming out, being able to be honest and talk openly with at least some work colleagues will help. Despite what people say about 'work is work' and 'your personal life is your personal life' it's never like that in practice. Humans are inquisitive animals, and the less you say about yourself, the more curious others seem to become. What's more, people do talk about their personal lives at work; they talk about what they did at the weekend, about their 'other halves', about divorces and affairs. Work parties often include an invitation to 'bring your partner or spouse' – whom, of course, everyone presumes to be of the opposite sex.

There are a number of options about coming out at work:

★ You can come out from the start, on your application form and at your interview, and then to all your colleagues when you are appointed. This is happening more and more frequently as large organisations adopt equal opportunities policies which include lesbians and gay men. Being out from the beginning has a number of advantages: if you have been working in a voluntary or paid capacity with a lesbian or gay organisation you can include this experience on your application form – and you don't have to consider the consequences of coming out, or being 'found out' some time later in your career.

> I came out on my application form. If they didn't want me working for them because I am lesbian, then I didn't want the job. My lesbianism is too much a part of me for me to even think about going back into the closet. They appointed me, but they do kind of treat me as the 'token gay' and pass everything about lesbians and gay men on to me. I've started passing it back, they need to deal with it.

> I'm very out at work. I haven't made a statement or anything, I just haven't hidden anything. If people ask me what I did at the weekend, or who I live with, then I tell them.

★ You can come out selectively once you're in a job. There are two options here: to come out to those colleagues with whom you are friendly and/or come out to a sympathetic manager or superviser.

Coming out to people you like is probably an easier topic to deal with, and many of the suggestions which are applicable to family and friends make sense here as well. Being guarded, and afraid to get involved in any discussions with work mates will not only increase your stress level at work, but it may make you feel isolated and unsupported:

> I told the woman I shared an office with. She knew that I was a feminist, and it just seems a progression from there. She was very supportive and used to challenge the remarks that people made. It was good that a very obvious heterosexual was standing up for lesbian rights.

Coming out to a manager or superviser, especially if you have an equal opportunities policy at your place of work, can be reassuring. With a manager you can always have a chat 'in confidence' and sound out how supportive she/he will be in the future. Having supportive managers can make the work environment much more pleasant. For instance, asking for time off because your partner is in hospital is far less stressful if your manager already knows the situation.

Not coming out to anyone at work is another option. How this works in practice depends on what sort of job you do and how involved socially you are with your colleagues. If the general atmosphere is anti-lesbian or gay it is sometimes very depressing sitting silently through conversations while your work mates say all sorts of ignorant and untrue things about lesbians. There may also be the fear of being 'found out'.

> One woman I used to work with set herself up as the expert on lesbians and gay men because her mother had a gay male friend. I remember particularly when we were talking one lunch time and she said that she had never met 'a real live lesbian'. I couldn't help thinking 'if only you knew'.

> There's no way I could come out. I'm a play leader and work quite a lot with kids with disabilities. The parents would freak, it's not worth my job.

Considerations about not coming out at work are similar to not coming out to family and friends. In fact, the issues may overlap if you are working for a family business or a friend of the family.

Protection

There is no specific protection for lesbians (and gay men) under employment law; you can be sacked just because you are a lesbian. In cases where this has happened and which have gone to Industrial Tribunals, the employers' decision has been upheld. It is important, because of this, to know your rights and where to get advice and support.

Find out if your employer has an equal opportunities

policy and get a copy of it. Lesbians may be specifically mentioned or included under various euphemisms like 'sexuality' or 'sexual orientation'. This may not give you total protection if you are discriminated against, but at least you will have a course to follow within the organisation. It is also useful to know what the policy is about things like compassionate leave.

If the organisation which you are working for has a policy which includes lesbians (or sexuality/sexual orientation) it may be that you have protection through contract law. The organisation is in effect saying that it will not allow discrimination on the grounds of sexuality. If you subsequently face harassment/discrimination to the point where you feel you must resign then you may have grounds to claim 'constructive dismissal' (circumstances were such that you felt that you were made to leave although it was you who took the initiative.) The employers would have to compensate you because they did not fulfil their part of the contract (ensuring that you wouldn't be discriminated against.) This strategy hasn't been tried by lesbians or gay men (that's why the paragraph is full of 'maybes'), however there has been a positive ruling in a case brought against an employer who had a policy about sexual harassment by a woman who experienced harassment to the point where she felt that she had to resign.

Even if the organisation which you are working for doesn't have an equal opportunities policy which includes lesbians and gay men, the Trade Union for your area of work might. It's worth joining your union for a lot of reasons, not least because they will support you if you are discriminated against or face dismissal. Many Unions also have lesbian and gay groups where you can meet other lesbians and gay men and get support.

The more you know what your rights are at work the stronger you can be in the face of discriminatory or threatening actions. If you are having problems at work get in touch with the specialist organisations at the earliest possible stage. Lesbian and Gay Employment Rights (LAGER) is an organisation in London (see contact list) which has been set up to give advice, information and help to lesbians and gay men on employment (and unemployment) issues. There is an autonomous women's group within LAGER.

Employment rights

Although there are no specific laws preventing employers discriminating against lesbians (or gay men) there are a number of general statutory laws which give all employees protection. There are also laws which prevent discrimination on the grounds of gender/sex, marital status and race. Your rights include:

★ From your first pay day you are entitled to an itemised pay slip showing what deductions have been made from your pay.

★ After four weeks of employment you are entitled to one week's notice before you can be sacked. A week's pay may be given instead of notice. This doesn't apply if you are sacked for gross misconduct.

★ After you have been employed for thirteen weeks, you are entitled to a written contract of employment which should include the conditions of employment (things like holiday entitlement, hours of work, sick pay, length of notice, rate of pay etc.) Unions often negotiate these terms and conditions nationally for their members although there may be slight local variations.

★ After you have been working for six months you are entitled to request the reasons for being sacked in writing.

★ After two years employment you have the right to two weeks notice. You also have the right not to be unfairly dismissed. 'Unfair dismissal' is a misleading term. An industrial tribunal will judge if an individual has been unfairly dismissed, not by looking at whether dismissal was unfair to the sacked individual, but whether the employer acted within the 'range of reasonable responses' available to employers. The tribunal must ask if the dismissal was something no reasonable employer would do. This process is biased towards the employer and often reflects widely held anti-lesbian views.

★ After two years employment you will have a right to compensation if you are made redundant.

★ You also have rights which are not dependent upon how long you have worked for an employer. Discrimination on the grounds of race and sex is not allowed in the recruitment or selection process or in the work place. Also, you don't have to be sacked or resign to take a case of discrimination on these grounds to an industrial tribunal.

The Race Relations Act (1976) and The Sex Discrimination Act (1975)

Under these Acts it is unlawful to treat a woman less favourably than a man or to make any distinction on grounds of race. These laws apply in the areas of recruitment, training, education and in the provision of goods, facilities and services to members of the public. There are two types of discrimination identified in the Acts: direct discrimination and indirect discrimination. In the case of the Sex Discrimination Act, direct discrimination would occur if a woman was denied a job in favour of a man with inferior qualifications. An example of indirect discrimination would be setting an age limit of 25 for a training course, and thus effectively excluding women in their early twenties who may be bringing up children. Similar examples may be found under the Race Relations Act. The Acts are outlined below.

Under the Race Relations Act, discrimination occurs when, on grounds of race "a person is treated less favourably than others would be treated or is segregated from others (direct discrimination)" or "There is apparently equal treatment in that a requirement or condition is applied to all people but the number of people of a particular racial group who can comply with it is proportionally smaller than the number of people outside that racial group who can comply and:

i) the employer cannot justify the requirement or condition as necessary for the job regardless of racial origin, and

ii) not being able to comply puts the person at a disadvantage (indirect discrimination.)"

An example of direct discrimination would be if a black employee on the same grade as other workers in an office was allocated all the boring, routine tasks while white employees were given more interesting and challenging tasks.

Indirect discrimination might occur if an employer demanded a higher standard of spoken English than the job required, and thereby precluded anyone for whom English was only a second language from applying.

Under the Sex Discrimination Act, discrimination against a woman occurs if "on the grounds of her sex, she is treated less favourably than a man is treated (direct discrimination)" or a requirement or condition is applied, or would apply equally to a man but "which is such that the proportion of women who can comply with it is considerably smaller than the proportion of men who can comply with it, and which cannot be shown to be justifiable irrespective of the sex of the person to whom it is applied, and which is to the detriment of a woman because she cannot comply with it (indirect discrimination.)"

In addition, it is unlawful to discriminate against a married person of either sex. A person is discriminated against if "on the grounds of his or her marital status he treats them less favourably than he treats an unmarried person of the same sex, or he applies to that person a requirement or condition which is applied or would be applied to an unmarried person but which is such that the proportion of married persons who can comply with it is considerably smaller than the proportion of unmarried persons of the same sex who can comply with it, and which cannot be shown to be justifiable irrespective of the marital status of the person to whom it is applied, and which is to that person's detriment because s/he cannot comply with it."

What to do

If you suffer discrimination at work either directly because you are a lesbian, or if you are discriminated against because you are a woman, or black you don't just have to sit there and take it. You may find support from the law, from Trades Unions and/or from specialist lesbian advice agencies.

If you think you are being discriminated against at work seek advice (for instance from LAGER or Lesbian Employment Rights) at the earliest possible stage. The things to keep in mind are:

★ Keep a written record of all the actions or incidents. Make a note of the date, time and circumstances and also who else was around, if anyone.

★ Don't agree to significant changes in your contract of employment without seeking advice.

★ Don't take action against your employer without getting advice first. For instance don't walk out of your job or resign, it's much harder to make a case if you have left the job apparently of your own free will. Also keep in mind that you probably won't be eligible to claim social security benefits for the first twenty-six weeks after resigning from a job.

★ If you are sacked get legal advice and contact your Trade Union shop steward immediately. Time is often an important factor in legal proceedings.

Conclusion

Coming out as a lesbian at your place of work carries with it both advantages and risks; you may face harassment, isolation or even be sacked. However, many organisations and Trades Unions are adopting positive equal opportunities policies which include lesbians and gay men and which acknowledge the sort of discrimination lesbians suffer and try to address these issues. Coming out in a supportive work atmosphere means that you can mention the skills you may have from voluntary work with lesbian groups or projects; you may find supportive employee groups within your workplace; you can challenge myths and stereotypes by just being there and you can, perhaps, provide a positive role model for other women who have not yet come to terms with their sexuality.

5: FINDING LESBIAN FRIENDS

Finding other lesbians to talk to about your feelings is an important and positive next step. When you meet other lesbians for the first time you will realise that not all of us fit the stereotyped images which are encouraged in the press. Lesbians are as varied a group as any in society, both physically and in their outlook and beliefs:

> When I first came to London I was fairly sure that I was a lesbian but I still had this idea that all other lesbians were very butch. My ideas were changed in one afternoon when a gay male friend of mine convinced me to go on the Gay Pride March. I spent the whole afternoon with my eyes and my mouth open. I couldn't believe that all the women there were lesbian – and that lesbians came in every size, shape, age and colour. Some were holding hands or kissing (in public!), some were pushing prams, some in wheelchairs. It was wonderful. I didn't have the courage to speak to anyone on that day, but it gave me the confidence to go to lesbian groups and clubs.

Because lesbians are such a diverse group, finding someone who has had similar experiences to your own may not be as difficult as you think. The support that you can get from someone who has been in a similar situation to yourself and survived to feel confident and positive about themselves, can be most reassuring:

When Lesbian Line suggested that I go to the young lesbian group I nearly fainted. Firstly because I didn't know that such groups existed, and secondly because I was scared shitless. I phoned the group to find out a bit more, and before I put the phone down I had arranged to meet someone who would take me to the next meeting. I thought about not turning up, but I did, and I am glad I did. Looking back I'm only sorry that I didn't know about it sooner. I found that I got a sympathetic ear when I talked about the reactions of parents and family. I couldn't even consider discussing those things with my straight friends.

Whether you're planning to come out to your parents, leave your husband or break up with your lover, you can get a lot of support by talking to other lesbians who have faced similar crises. They won't have all the answers, but you might be able to pick up a few useful suggestions and, maybe, learn from their mistakes.

Coming out is the other thing we all, as lesbians, have in common. It's likely to have been a difficult experience for most women who will remember the pain and uncertainty that had to be faced. These women will usually be happy to help others get through where they can.

A common feeling for lesbians who are first coming to terms with their sexuality is that they are 'the only one in the world' who has these 'freakish' desires. Such is their isolation and sense of guilt that they become convinced that nobody else knows what it means to be attracted to a member of the same sex. The mere discovery that there are thousands of others who feel the same way can provide a validation, a reassurance and a great confidence boost.

Finding lesbian friends and lesbian places is often a welcome relief for many women. There is something relaxing about being in a bookshop, cafe or club or pub where you don't have to worry about what you say and don't have to be constantly on guard in case you show affection to a friend or partner. It's good to be able to ask for the magazines or books you want without wondering what the sales person is thinking. Like the relief of acknowledging who and what you are when you come out to yourself, making friends brings with it a relief of BEING who you are. There is always the added possibility (if you're looking for a partner) that Ms Right will be among the women you are meeting.

So meeting other lesbians is important for validation, confidence and support. However, for many women – especially those who come out without knowing other lesbians or gay men, or in a small town where there are no lesbian or gay clubs or groups – this can be one of the most frightening steps forward. It is also one of the most important.

How do you meet other lesbians?

Telephone your nearest Lesbian Line or Gay Switchboard and find out what's going on in your area. If you live in a big city you may well have a reasonable choice of activities. Smaller towns offer less of a variety – if any thing at all – and you may have to travel. Relocation to an area where there is more opportunity to meet other lesbians and find a satisfying social life might seem like a big step, but if you are living in a rural setting with no opportunities to explore your feelings with other people you might have little choice.

Groups

Discussion or support groups for women who are just coming out are a good way to meet other lesbians. I would suggest that, if possible, you start with one of these. They are important because the emphasis is on talking, sharing and supporting each other. There is usually no pressure to say anything unless you feel like it. If there is anyone with whom you feel you might 'click', then don't hesitate to approach them – perhaps making a comment about the evening's discussion. This will provide the 'hook' on which to hang further initiatives. After all, most of the other women at the group will be there for the same reason you are – to find friends.

However careful the organisers are to create a friendly atmosphere, most people find situations like this daunting. There is the constant fear of rejection, particularly in those who are lacking confidence to start with. To make a first approach can, therefore, be very difficult. Unfortunately there is little alternative; take your courage in both hands and plunge in. Don't be discouraged by the occasional failure to 'hit it off' – keep trying, and eventually you'll get what you want. If you feel shyness is a big problem for you, there are several excellent books available on the subject which give suggestions for overcoming it. Most people are shy to an extent, it's just that some are better than others at showing a confident front to the world.

There are also groups for women from different racial or cultural backgrounds, Black, Chinese, Jewish, Irish lesbian groups and many more. There are groups for Catholic lesbians, lesbians with disabilities, lesbian mothers, young lesbians, older lesbians. All of these groups provide a safe and relaxed atmosphere in which to meet and talk to others.

Another sort of group which you might consider is one that is organising an event or campaign. If you are happier where the emphasis is on doing rather than talking, these might suit you better. Most groups like this welcome volunteers whether or not they have special skills, like typing or graphics. Volunteers who are happy to stuff and stick envelopes, or who can drive a mini bus are invaluable to such projects. Being involved in an activity such as this makes conversation much easier, and there is no need to make a big commitment until you are ready to do so.

The important thing about groups is that they bring you into contact with other lesbians, which is an essential beginning. Women from these groups often organise outings to clubs or events, or give their own parties. Go to as many of these events as you can manage and in this way your increased social opportunities will soon bring you a circle of lesbian friends. It's surprising how reassuring it can be to walk into a club or pub and see familiar faces you have met at groups, even if you haven't talked to them before. You will probably be surprised too, that after a couple of weeks or months, you will become one of the 'familiar faces' yourself, with whom new members of the group will identify.

Courses

Attending a course specially aimed at lesbians, or women in general, can be an excellent way to make contact with other lesbians. The courses can range from lesbian history evening classes to photography courses to one-day conferences of particular interest to lesbians. Unfortunately, such courses are mainly a luxury of the large cities, but they are becoming more popular so it's always worth checking what your local opportunities might be. Generally, the smaller the group, and the longer the course runs, the better the chance of starting friendships.

Magazines

The personal columns or lonely hearts pages of some magazines are another way of making contact with other lesbians. Many women shy away from this kind of thing because there seems to be a taboo about admitting that you are isolated or lonely. But if you can overcome this taboo, personal ads can be a very effective way to find new friends. Having said that, it is important to emphasise that caution is required at first: always use a box number and try to make contact with respondents by telephone before you arrange to meet them in person. You can then assess how genuine the contact is – it is not unknown for cranks to use the advertisements to write obscene or abusive letters. For a happy-ever-after example I know none better than my own:

> When I was new to London I answered a couple of advertisements in one of the weekly listings magazines, having first had grave doubts about what sort of people would advertise. I'm glad I did. I met a lesbian couple who took me under their wing and showed me around the clubs. I then answered another advertisement and I met a woman with

whom I fell in love and eventually lived with for a number of years.

For women living in isolated villages this route may be one of the easiest for making contacts. You can establish a 'pen-pal' relationship which will be less expensive than travelling the countryside in search of groups and venues. Please try to be thoughtful about the people who reply. There may well be some answers which you immediately dismiss as unsuitable, but please try to write a short note to the respondent acknowledging her letter. After all, she has taken a big risk in replying to you, and it is only fair and courteous to reply, even if it is to say that you don't want to pursue the matter. If anyone sends photographs, please make sure you send them back – they can be quite expensive.

Pubs and clubs

For many lesbians their first point of contact with other lesbians is at a gay or lesbian pub or club. Nightclubs suit some people better than others. For those who enjoy music and dancing then finding the local lesbian or gay disco can revolutionise their lives. In the larger centres there is usually a lesbian only or lesbian and gay venue open most nights, and the range of music varies from disco to alternative. Even if nightclubs are not your first choice of entertainment, there is something uplifting about walking into a crowded club and realising that everyone there is a lesbian.

Nightclubs also have disadvantages, especially if you are new to the lesbian scene. They can be expensive, they tend to focus on alcohol, they are often smokey, but more importantly the volume of the music doesn't make it easy to have conversations. Few lesbian venues are wheelchair user accessible. Often, even if you can manoeuvre into the place, the toilets are inaccessible. There are a few exceptions, so if you have mobility difficulties telephone your local Lesbian Line to find out about access details.

In general, if you are going to a club by yourself, it will probably be up to you to take the initiative and begin to talk to other people, or ask other women to dance. Rejection or disinterest may not be aimed at you personally, but it can be very disillusioning. As with the other avenues, perseverance is the key word. If you are a nightclub sort of person, keep trying. Don't judge a place by only one or two visits.

Pubs and bars usually offer more of a variety of atmospheres, but few are lesbian only, even for one night a week. Initially the more popular bars might be worth visiting – there is more chance of someone starting a conversation in a crowded bar, even if it's only because they want to share your table. Again, if you go alone it will usually be up to you to initiate conversation. Once again, it needs courage to start with, but the more you practice, the easier it gets.

Nightclubs tend to focus on younger people, especially if they are exclusively lesbian. There are a few groups and venues which cater for older lesbians. These range from supper clubs (for lesbian professional and business women over 30), support groups and venues which have a quieter atmosphere and draw an older clientele.

Women's Centres and Lesbian and Gay Centres

Within the last ten years or so, there has been a growth of both women's centres and lesbian and gay centres. These are useful places to contact and visit.

Lesbian and Gay Centres in particular offer a range of events, activities, groups and support. Even if you are not going for a particular event, they usually have a cafe and/or bar facilities, stock the lesbian and gay newspapers and have a range of contacts and advertisements pinned on their noticeboards. Again, if you prefer to feel more actively involved, these centres are often on the lookout for volunteers. Working in the centre also means you have an 'excuse' to speak to anyone in the place!

Start your own group

If there are no groups in your area, or no group offering what you want, why not set up your own? Initially you will need time, energy and commitment but this usually pays off when others join and take on some of the responsibilities. If you do set up a group you will have control over how much commitment you are prepared to give it – you can choose to meet once a week or once a month. Having meetings in members homes is the cheapest alternative, but women's centres may be more than willing to offer you a room, and perhaps back-up and support as well. If there is a pub in your area which has supported lesbian and/or gay events in the past it may be possible to arrange to use one of their function rooms on a regular basis. Of course you may want to set up a group which doesn't need a meeting room – you could organise a group which plays football once a month, or goes swimming, or walking, or to the cinema; the options are infinite. It would be wise to organise a box number (enquire at the Post Office or British Monomarks in London) or other contact address rather than use your personal address; this avoids unwanted or inconvenient visits from strangers or even group members. If you are thinking of advertising and including your home telephone number, be prepared for hoax and abusive calls as well as calls from women who may be desperate for contact or advice. The more help you can get from other groups in the area the better. And if you do start a group don't forget to let the local Lesbian Line or Gay Switchboard know.

Move to the city

This sounds a bit desperate, but if you're feeling isolated (especially if your coming out as a lesbian has not been welcomed by family and friends) you may consider the option which many people take every year: move to a big city which offers more opportunities. This is not the easy way out. Pulling up your roots and heading for a strange place brings with it many complications. Housing and employment problems tend to be worse in large towns, and dealing with all of this without an established network of family and friends can be awesome. If you are planning to move to one of the larger cities, it would be worth getting in touch with the Lesbian Line or Gay Switchboard there to find out if they offer an accommodation service (flat share.) They can also tell you what groups exist and give any tips they may have for someone moving to their area.

6: LIFESTYLES AND RELATIONSHIPS

> Before I had a lesbian relationship I thought that I was content. I wasn't happy and I wasn't particularly unhappy. Then I discovered women. I didn't realise anything could be so wonderful. Now that I have something to compare my previous life with I realise I was merely existing. As a dyke things have opened my eyes, extended my feelings and raised my hopes.

Being lesbian means having a lifestyle for which we haven't been educated or prepared. There are no well-trodden tracks for us to follow as there are for heterosexual women; for them the sequence usually consists of boyfriends, getting engaged, getting married, moving out of home, having children, and so on. Even getting divorced is accepted into this sequence and there are laws about how this should happen, and agencies which try to prevent it happening. Heterosexual relationships have a pattern (which may vary slightly), and the acknowledgement in law that they exist. There are tax concessions for married men, there are alimony responsibilities, there are joint insurance policies and joint memberships to other organisations (eg. AA or RAC.)

Lesbians don't have the same set of expectations; this means there are more options but fewer role models. Like other areas in our lives, there is no single answer and no 'right' one. In a strange way, this lack of 'rules' makes it both harder and easier to make decisions about how we want to live. As women, we are probably in a position to make choices which may be denied to our heterosexual sisters. But, as we discovered when coming out, making decisions isn't always easy or straightforward.

The first set of choices is available to most young people (lesbian or not): we can live alone, we can live with friends or we can live with partners. Just as many heterosexual people will chose to live with friends who are heterosexual, many lesbians chose to live with lesbian friends. For many lesbians who have moved away from their home town, or are estranged from their families, this sort of living arrangement often gives them an alternative 'family' for support. Having flatmates who are lesbian means that talking about relationships or where to go on a Saturday night starts from a common assumption and perspective:

> Sylvie and I are friends. She had a spare room in her flat so I moved in. We don't fancy each other, but we get along really well and have fun when we go out, and it's great to have someone to go to clubs with.

Some of the lesbians who live with friends have stable relationships with other women who may chose to live in other circumstances. Living separately from our partner is one of the choices we have. A whole range of types of relationships are open to lesbians and this may influence who we chose to live with.

Some lesbians choose to live a 'separatist' lifestyle, (ie. separate from men.) They aim to ensure that all their energy is spent on women. Sometimes separatism is more of an attitude towards life – women live and work in cities or towns where they come into contact with men, but in the areas where they have control and choice, they choose to be with women, or spend their money on services provided by women. Some women have women-only homes where it is agreed that no men will be invited. Separatism in this sense is based more on realism (the meter reader may be a man), but some women do manage to live a more ideal separatist lifestyle in rural rather than urban settings.

Types of relationships

We can choose to be celibate: for most people this means not having sexual relationships with other people. It can be a very positive choice, although most would view it as a space between relationships. There is no reason why we have to be constantly sexually active just because that is the way the media portrays us. Celibacy is a choice which reflects that we have control over our own bodies and lives, it also means that we have a choice to resume sexual activity should our circumstances change in the future. Celibacy does not imply lack of emotional involvement, or stopping affectionate relationships. It can be a conscious choice, and doesn't have to be regarded as a punishment.

We can choose to have a relationship with one person exclusively. These are called monogamous relationships, the 'mono' meaning 'one'. Monogamous relationships are the ones that we are most accustomed to seeing – marriage is based on this format. One researcher has concluded that the present Christian marriage vows are in fact based on vows which two people of the same sex used to take in early Christendom.[1] While some might say that lesbian monogamy simply tries to ape heterosexual relationships, there can be substantial differences, which we will explore later in the chapter.

> I was 38 when I fell in love with Marion. I felt like a teenager again. I still do to some extent, but that's because I'm still madly and passionately in love with her.

We can choose to be non-monogamous. This means having more than one partner. There are different types of non-monogamy – you can have two or more equal relationships,

1. 'Gays were the first to wed – professor claims.' *Capital Gay,* 9th August 1985. Report on Research by Yale professor John Boswell. The research by a Yale History Professor suggests that gay marriages were celebrated several centuries before the development of heterosexual marriage rites.

or you can have a primary relationship with secondary affairs. The latter is probably fairly close to the heterosexual concept of the 'open' marriage where both partners agree to permit partners outside of the relationship.

Roles in relationships

One of the areas where lesbian relationships differ from heterosexual relationships is that they don't start off with an automatic power imbalance. In our society men have more power and status than women, and this is reflected in the institution of marriage – men are traditionally regarded as being the head of the household. Attitudes and laws have changed, and continue to change, but until the turn of the century, women were thought of as the property of men, whether it was their father or their husband. By fighting for the right to vote, the suffragettes won the right of women to have a say in how the country was governed.

When two women have a relationship, neither comes into it with any more assumed power than the other. There are of course other issues of power which exist in this society and need to be challenged: older people have more power than young people (but the elderly have little power), white people have more power than black people, and able-bodied people have more power than the disabled. However, as far as the gender issue is concerned, women potentially start off equal.

It follows that there are no expected roles. A popular misconception is that in a lesbian relationship, one woman will play the male (butch) role and the other will play the female (femme) role. Although there are, undeniably, relationships which do operate on this basis, the trend in recent years is to share tasks, not according to perceived roles, but on a more equal basis:

When I first realised I was a lesbian all the women seemed to be playing roles. One was 'butch' and wore the trousers (literally), the other was femme and played the role of 'wife'. I didn't want to be restricted to just do or be done to. I felt initially

67

that having at last identified what I was, I didn't fit in. I caused a few waves and scandals in those days, but as you can see, everything worked out.

A common question heterosexuals ask lesbians is 'who plays the man?' or, more subtly, 'who does the cooking?' (They also assume that one of the women 'plays the role of the man' in bed.)

This lack of defined gender roles seems to result in a lesser degree of guilt and duty than I have observed in some heterosexual relationships. If something isn't done – whether it's making the tea or cleaning the car – it's not because either of the women has neglected her 'duty', but rather because the couple haven't decided who will take responsibility for the task that day. Whilst heterosexual couples have to deal with the fear of labels such as 'bad housewife' or 'incompetent husband', any criticism of a lesbian couple will be levelled at both of them.

Lesbians living together as a couple, therefore, have the opportunity of starting from scratch. Chores can be shared in alternating periods: ('you cook this week, I'll cook next week,') they could be done together: ('If you're making the lasagne, I'll do a salad to go with it,') or they could be divided: ('Whilst you're cooking, I'll make a start on the ironing.') They can be negotiated in many other ways too. The main thing is that neither is expected to do a particular task simply because she is a woman.

Lesbian relationships

Whichever variation of relationship you choose, you will need to make your views clear to partners. Choosing a monogamous relationship to begin with doesn't mean you must have monogamous relationships throughout your life. Types of relationships may change with partners or over time. However, unless you discuss what your hopes and commitments are at the outset of the relationship, you are likely to end up having the discussion under far more emotional and heated circumstances later. Be honest and negotiate about the ground rules. If you are seeing someone else, and want to continue to have non-monogamous relationships, be sure that both partners are aware of this before one or both get hurt. Similarly, if you prefer monogamous relationships, you need to make this clear at the start of the relationship. If it's not spoken about then you may end up with a lot of hurt when the love of your life sleeps with someone else.

Making relationships work

There are a few simple things to keep in mind which seem to help a relationship work:

★ Know the ground rules: don't expect to be able to change strong feelings about monogamy or non-monogamy. This also applies to other aspects of relationships. If a potential partner has, for example, a drinking or gambling habit, beware of entering a relationship thinking that you will be able to change her. Maybe you can, but be realistic in your assessment.

★ Be honest and talk. If you both can talk about all sorts of things, in bed and out, there is less chance of misunderstandings. Don't be afraid of having disagreements or arguments. Keeping things bottled up inside often leads to much more explosive anger later. However, if you do argue, try to avoid saying hurtful things which you don't mean, don't bring her family into arguments just to score points. There is also something to be said for the old adage 'never let the sun go down on an argument'. Remember that you can agree to disagree. The latter option is useful if you have different opinions, but it's not useful if you are talking about the terms of your relationship. Finding space to cool off – perhaps by taking a walk – is a useful way to help get things into perspective. However, these should be positive and explained: ('I'm just going out for a walk, I need some time to think things through') not negative and aggressive – slamming out in a sulk without saying where you are going just creates more tension.

★ Trust each other. This is made easier if you talk honestly and both of you understand and accept the terms of your relationship.

★ Accept that both of you will want to spend time with other people. This may include work colleagues, family or friends. As they say, no woman is an island, and if you trust each other and view these times apart as adding to your relationship, there should be no friction.

★ Try and spend 'positive' time together. Your partner shouldn't only see you when you are exhausted or troubled. Make time all through your relationship to have 'dates' or 'dirty weekends.' If you are a romantic, keep it up. Flowers or cards, or remembering your anniversaries helps to strengthen and reinforce relationships.

★ Be sensitive to each others needs and emotions. If your partner suffers from pre-menstrual tension – which might surface as being weepy or just generally 'scratchy' – try to make allowances for it. When two women live together, or spend a lot of time together, their periods often coincide. Recognise mood changes if they occur in both of you.

★ Keep ex-lovers out of any discussion about the relationship you are presently in. There's not much harm in informing your partner about your history, but it never seems to help to go into specific details about sexual exploits or practice. Such reminiscences don't add anything to current relationships and may result in your partner wondering if you are making uncomplimentary comparisons. There might also be the insecurity of your partner wondering what you ll say about her should you break up.

★ It is not weakness to occasionally need, and to ask for, support. For example if you're unemployed and your partner isn't she may offer to pay for something. Don't rush to refuse, however bad you may feel about it: think how you would feel if the situations were reversed. Just remember, whatever the issue, the roles may well change at another point in your relationship.

★ Don't bring your work home if you can possibly help it.

A lot of these hints are just common sense, but somehow it is easy to lose sight of them when a relationship isn't working. There's also the old saying 'start as you mean to go on'. In relationships this is particularly important. It's much easier to sort things out at the beginning than trying to resolve them in a crisis.

Money and finances

One of the differences between lesbian and heterosexual relationships is that ours are not acknowledged in law. This has implications for women who live together or are in a committed relationship. It may sound a bit mercenary or pessimistic to sort out finances and wills early in the relationship, but in the long term written agreements may help avoid arguments and wrangling later. Getting things down on paper will be especially important for women who buy a house or flat, furnishings, a car or any major item together.

If you and your partner decide to live together, you need to discuss not only your attitudes to money but how, in practice, you are going to run your household. Situations may change, but you need to talk about such things as: does one of you earn more than the other, is one of you unemployed? Does one or both of you have children? There are three basic options:

★ Completely joint finances: both partners' money goes into a joint account for keeping the debts paid and the relationship solvent.

★ A joint account to cover mutual out-goings, and separate personal accounts for any money either earns beyond the needs of the first account.

★ Proportional input, where each bill is paid either according to money coming in – eg 'I earn twice as much as my partner, therefore I will pay two-thirds of all the bills', or according to how much one partner uses a resource or clocks up expenditure. For example if a couple buy a car together, and one of them uses it for work every day, the driver may pay more towards the car.

There are many variations of how women sort out finances; to some extent this reflects the many types of relationships which lesbians have. There is no 'correct' answer, but each relationship needs to agree its terms as soon as possible. Probably the best choice is the solution which is least complicated for your particular circumstances.

If you are investing in something expensive together, for example a home, you need to agree what is going to happen if one of you wants to move out. Not talking about possible eventualities doesn't mean they won't happen. Decide what you want to do and then get some legal advice about formalising it. This course of action is particularly important when you're buying something together that is only legally in one partner's name. Make sure your joint ownership is noted and think about what is going to happen if one of you wants out, or if one can't keep up payments.

Of course it is not only when relationships break down that women can regret not making some kind of formalised plan for their finances. For example, if your partner dies intestate (without making a will) you will have no legal right to her property. This will probably go to her family as legal next of kin. Making a last will and testament is not – as some people superstitiously believe – inviting disaster, but it could help prevent one. This issue will be dealt with in more detail in the legal chapter.

Other considerations

When you have a relationship with someone it's usually not

simply you and her; each of you will have other special people in your lives. It could be friends, ex-lovers, parents or children. These 'external' relationships need to be accepted and respected. If you are going to relate to any of these people as a couple then you will have to be honest with them about your love and the nature of your relationship. If they know that you are a lesbian couple then visits won't be spoiled by the stress of possible discovery. You won't have to remove every trace of your lifestyle before they come to call!

> Mary and I had been living together for over two years when her parents came to visit. It was awful, not her parents visiting, but having to check every bookshelf, every photograph album, every piece of paper in the place. We moved half of our stuff into the spare room even though it was her parents who were going to be sleeping there. We were so tense in the anticipation, and so relieved and convinced that we had done a thorough job that we completely missed seeing a pile of gay newspapers we had gathered up and forgotten to lock away. They saw them during their first cup of tea. Mary nearly fainted, but in the end it was OK, they had guessed anyway. All that re-arranging for nothing.

There may of course be special people whose presence is not just confined to occasional visits. If one or both partners have children, their needs will have to be carefully considered – particularly if they are young and still dependent upon their mothers. If you don't have children but your partner does, you will need to accept from the beginning the special relationship which exists between mother and child. Children will need to spend positive time just with their mother, and sometimes you will be the outsider who may be perceived as a threat to the time, love and attention which the child might regard as exclusively hers or his. With careful handling – perhaps over a long period – this seldom results in any major problems and very strong relationships can develop between children and their mother's lesbian partner.

Very successful co-parenting arrangements have resulted between two women.

Parenting

Although many women have children from past heterosexual relationships, it is possible to decide to have children once you are in a lesbian relationship. This is also an option for lesbians outside relationships, too. The choices open to heterosexuals are getting pregnant, fostering or adoption. All these avenues are open to lesbians, too, to a greater or lesser extent.

★ Biological motherhood: One or both partners could decide to become pregnant at some time in their relationship. It seems that the best method of getting pregnant is through D.I. (Donor Insemination). This procedure involves the introduction of sperm into the woman's vagina when she is at her most fertile. It's a very simple procedure, so simple in fact that many lesbians in the past have arranged for a sperm donation from a male friend or contact and then carried it out themselves. It may not be advisable to do this at the moment because of the possibility of coming into contact with HIV (the virus associated with Aids) which can be present in sperm. Artificial insemination is sometimes available to single women and out lesbians through medical clinics (where sperm donations are tested for HIV before use) and it would be advisable to telephone Lesbian Line to get advice on the best and nearest clinic to you.

★ Intercourse with a man: the sexual intercourse may just be for the purpose of getting pregnant, but many women have found this degrading and traumatic. There are also dangers: HIV infection (or other sexually transmitted diseases), or of the man making claims on the child if he finds out about it.

★ Fostering: Some local authorities have a policy of not discriminating against lesbians who wish to foster and it may be worth finding out about the position at your local Council on this issue. Be warned – whilst some local councils are moving towards an equal opportunities policy, others remain very anti-lesbian. Although it is possible to foster as a 'single woman' it is probably better for both you and the child if you can be open.

★ Adoption: This is more difficult, primarily because the process is dealt with through the courts and both the law and judges are not renowned for their progressive ideas. However, there have been successful cases of lesbians being granted rights to adopt. Adoption has been permitted where the child is considered 'hard to place', usually meaning a child with severe physical disabilities or learning difficulties, or both.

An important point to bear in mind is that with all of these avenues, only one woman will have legal rights over the child or children. The non-biological mother will have no claims to caring for a child even if her partner dies. The legal system only allows a single person or a married heterosexual couple to adopt. This is one of the points which you should keep in mind when drawing up your will.

Dealing with breaking up

Even fairy tale romances don't always end happily ever after. Some people grow apart, some just never really got on in the first place but couldn't see beyond the initial thrill. Sometimes one partner falls out of love, or perhaps in love with someone else. A million reasons could be cited for why some relationships don't last forever. Just because you are in a lesbian relationship doesn't mean that all the problems disappear. Do be careful not to blame your lesbianism for broken relationships. Your sexuality is not, in itself, likely to be the reason for a broken heart – after all, heterosexuals frequently break-up/divorce/separate, too.

But it's a sad fact that relationships do break-up. The important thing is to survive the trauma, learn from your experiences and get back to the business of living and loving as soon as you can. Breaking up with someone is about dealing with loss. You have to grieve for that loss, it hurts but it's not fatal. Again, there are some common sense things to bear in mind:

★ Try to sort out all joint matters as soon as you can after you decide to split. Dragging out money quarrels for months has often just led to increased bad feeling.

★ If things aren't working, a quick, clean break will be less painful in the long run, even if it hurts more in the short term.

★ Your life may seem empty and unhappy after the split, but if you can manage not to have contact with your ex-lover for a while, then your healing process will be quicker. Seeing her too soon after a split may bring back all the emotions of the break-up and reopen the wound.

★ Talk about your feelings with friends, but don't try to make mutual friends take sides, and do respect them if they continue to see both of you as individuals. If you feel isolated, phone a Lesbian Line. Talking often helps get things into perspective.

★ Writing down how you feel and what you are going through also often helps to heal.

★ Resist the urge to 'drown your sorrows' or numb them with tranquillisers. The problems don't go away – they'll still be there unresolved when you've sobered up. Face up to them and accept the pain as inevitable and the price of being human.

★ Don't expect to move straight from being lovers to being friends; but it often happens after a healing period. Don't burden her, or yourself, with too many expectations.

★Try to avoid apportioning blame. It takes two to make a relationship.

★ Be optimistic. If the relationship wasn't meant to be, then it's better to accept that. Perhaps you had to break up because you were destined for a relationship with a wonderful woman who is waiting just around the corner.

★ 'Time heals' is a truism which you should keep to the front of your mind during the bad times.

Conclusion

Lesbian relationships come in many varieties. Like any relationship they need to be worked at. Sometimes they end in heartache, often they last for decades. Each woman will need to explore which kind of relationship suits her best.

7: SEX AND SENSUALITY

Female sexuality is often seen as reactive and responsive. As women we are judged in terms of maleness and male sexuality and women who don't fit the stereotype of passiveness become (in men's terms) slags or sluts. Because of this idea of maleness being central to sex, some people find it difficult to imagine that two women can have a satisfying sex life together. Men in particular will say that a woman has turned to lesbianism because she hasn't found the right man – or more particularly 'she hasn't met me yet'.

The question of what lesbians do in bed can be a scary one for the inexperienced. 'I couldn't go to bed with a woman', they might say, 'I wouldn't know what to do'. The main thing to remember is that being a lesbian is not just about performing sexual acts with another woman, it's about having a relationship – whether that lasts a night or a decade. Sex is important, but it's not everything, and usually the way you relate outside of bed will have an effect on how you get on in bed. If you can be honest and open then your chances of having good sex are increased.

One of the general problems women have with sex is that any education they may have received will probably have concentrated on the biological and reproductive aspects. It is only fairly recently that biology books have begun to include the clitoris in diagrams of female sex organs or genitalia. This was because the clitoris was not seen has having a 'function' – not in the mechanics of reproduction, anyway. As most women have discovered, it has a very important role in the achievement of pleasure and orgasm. As the sex researcher Kinsey pointed out in *Sexual Behaviour of the Human Female* [1], we have a great capacity for sexual pleasure which is not connected with reproduction; masturbation is a good example of this.

So, what do lesbians do in bed? Well, before we look in detail at that question, you should remind yourself that as a woman you have a head start when the topic is sex with other women. There might not be many sex manuals around, but you already know the territory. By masturbating and exploring your own body you will already have an idea of what feels good, and how you might make other women feel good, too.

However, if you feel bad about yourself or about your body or genitals, you may find it difficult to accept that other women might find you attractive. If your self-image is negative it could be hard to imagine that other women could want to make love to you and give you pleasure. This may be an important issue for women with disabilities, especially in a society which places an emphasis on body-beautiful and physical attractiveness. It is important for all of us to remember that our sexuality is about more than simply who we fancy, it's about our attitudes, priorities and politics. Our sexuality is about who we are; sex is about what we do. So, before we start talking about making love with a partner, let's talk about loving ourselves.

In the same way that we rarely hear or see anything positive in the straight world about lesbianism, we rarely hear or see anything positive about our bodies, and especially our genitals. We learn that our genitals should be hidden, that we are not supposed to touch them, that they are ugly. We hear words which refer to those parts of our bodies being used as terms of abuse. Anything associated with female genitalia – such as periods – is seen as distasteful. Just look at the way TV advertising approaches the subject of tampons. In these ads, which are strictly controlled by the TV authorities, there is no direct mention of what is being advertised or what the product is for. The advertisements seem to be about sky diving or swimming. We could be led to think that women with disabilities don't have periods, although the menstrual cycle is often unaffected by

1. *Sexual Behaviour in the Human Female* A. C. Kinsey et al. (W.B.Saunders Company, Philadelphia and London, 1953)

disability. Menstruation is, after all, a natural function of women's bodies – the fact that it is apparently regarded with disgust by society at large indicates the depth of taboo associated with women's genitals. We grow up in a world which degrades and objectifies women, which treats lesbians as perverts. We already know that a lot of what is said about lesbians is completely wrong. The same applies to what is said about women's bodies and about lesbian sex.

One of the first issues which we raised in this book was about words. This is also an issue when we are talking about our bodies and sex. In most books and sex manuals, technical or biological words such as vagina and labia are used. In everyday life most people tend not to use these words; they have others to refer to the sexual parts of their bodies: cunt, fanny, private parts, tits, breasts, to name but a few. In this chapter I have chosen to use the word cunt. Although it is often used in an abusive way, we can reclaim it and give it different and more positive connotations. This has already been done with the words lesbian and dyke. When we deliberately choose such words to describe ourselves, we rob them of their negative meanings.

If you feel happier with other words, just read this chapter and replace the words I use with the ones you feel more comfortable with.

Getting to know yourself

Most women know what they look like and are familiar with their image in the mirror. But how many of us only look for and notice the things we don't like? Many women spend an inordinate amount of time trying to make their bodies conform to a standard set by men and the fashion market. They fail to appreciate who they are and what they have to offer and they miss the pleasure of being unique. The next time you stand naked in front of a mirror look at yourself positively. The curve of your belly, the shape of your breasts, the lines on your neck, they are the features which make you into your own, inimitable self and which will, when combined with other parts of your personality, attract other women.

Liking yourself

Plan time for yourself when there's going to be no one else around. Forget about the ironing or the washing up from last night and spoil yourself; make a cup of tea, play your favourite music. Relax in a bath, treat yourself to bubbles or bath oil if you can get your hands on some. As you wash yourself, concentrate on your body, making a mental note of the parts you really like. Afterwards wrap yourself in your fluffiest towel and find a comfortable, warm place where you won't be disturbed – your bedroom, perhaps. Now, closing your eyes, go through the inventory of things you liked about your body. Most of us can find a few things we like about our bodies: the feel of our skin, the little soft hairs on our forearms, our lips, eyes or eyebrows, the shape of our toes – anything. Now spend some more time touching these bits, and perhaps finding other parts you like.

Now pay some special attention to your cunt, whether it was on your list of good bits or not. Find a hand mirror and arrange it so that you can have a really good look at yourself. Try to see it in the terms that other women have described it: a flower with soft petals opening out around the bud of a clitoris. Feel the textures, look at the colours. Every woman is unique; get to know yourself and love yourself. Some women worry because they think that their genitals are misshapen, that their cunt lips too large or too small or that things aren't arranged the way that they are in diagrams in text books. But remember, such diagrams are generalisations and photographs can only show one image type. No two cunts are alike, but each is as beautiful as another in its own way. This is just another part of our uniqueness, our different shaped or coloured cunts simply are as they are, there is no question of worse or better.

Now experiment with what feels good. Caress yourself, your shoulders, the back of your neck, your breasts, your stomach, your thighs. Now move on to your cunt. Change the speed and pressure of your strokes, touch every part. If you are used to masturbating, you should already be familiar with your cunt. Even so, take time to really explore. Taste the lubricating juice your cunt produces. If you orgasm, think

81

about how it felt. (Don't worry if you don't, it's a bonus, not the aim).

Don't just stop there. Go over all the things you like again, put them all together and think of yourself as a whole, as a sum of the parts.

Masturbating

Masturbating is very common – there are very few people who haven't done it at some stage in their lives. Despite the myths you might have heard, masturbation is not harmful physically, emotionally or sexually. As with other sexual matters, the fact that men do it is well known; it's even accepted that male friends might masturbate together. However, female masturbation is discussed far less frequently.

For many of us, our first sexual arousal is self-arousal. Some women have masturbated for as long as they can remember, others begin later, having had to cope with parental or religious taboos and warnings. The guilt and fear of punishment or exposure often impedes our finding pleasure from our own bodies. There is also the line of thought which implies that we are only masturbating because we can't get the 'real thing' – i.e. sex with men. This, too, is fatuous. Masturbating is about pleasing ourselves, when and how we want to. Masturbating occurs both within and outside sexual relationships; it can form part of lovemaking, as well as being an adjunct to relationships. Masturbating is also often linked with fantasies and using sex toys like vibrators. Again, there is nothing uncommon about this. If we talked about our experience more with other women this would soon become clear.

Making love to a woman

So, we're back to the question of what lesbians do in bed. A lesbian who was 'soap-boxing' at Speakers Corner in Hyde

Park, London was asked by a male heckler about what women do together in bed, her answer is useful:

'The same as you, but longer and better.'

Women usually find foreplay – the touching and caressing part of sex – essential. Women are quite capable of having multiple orgasms, so sex can last for as long as you like. That's one of the reasons I've called this chapter sex and sensuality: lesbian sex is not wham-bam-thank-you-ma'am, roll over and snore (as some women have described sex with men). Perhaps, therefore, it's a good thing that there isn't a proliferation of sex manuals dealing with lesbian sex. It means that women do experiment more and talk about what they like, or what they want to try. Again, it needs to be said that there is no right way or wrong way to 'perform' lesbian sex. You need to discover what you like having done to you, and what you like to do to your partner. You're less likely to go wrong if you talk about things and experiment:

> The first time she touched me I felt like a sparkler set alight. It was an intimate, but not sexual touch – she ran her fingers softly down my cheek. When we eventually made love I felt like a whole fireworks display.

> The best thing, well one of the best things about being a dyke, is talking. Really communicating. And affection, of course. We're both very 'cuddly' people.

Now we can consider some of the sexual practices that lesbians use. This is far from an exhaustive guide, and not every lesbian will enjoy doing all these things. Don't worry if you're enjoying some activities which aren't covered in this section, it probably just means that you are imaginative beyond the scope of this book. It's up to you to decide what you want to try, and there is no rule to say that you have to enjoy everything. It's all a matter of personal preference.

For women with disabilities, communication and experimentation may be of particular importance. People with disabilities are seldom seen as being sexual, let alone being lesbian. Much of what has been published dealing with sex for people with disabilities approaches it in a very traditional and heterosexual way. Women can still experience orgasms even when a significant part of their bodies are without sensation or motion. There is no reason why lesbians with disabilities shouldn't engage in any sexual activity which is physiologically possible, pleasurable and acceptable to her and her partner. Sexual encounters can have a profound impact on our sense of self-esteem, and this is equally true for women with disabilities who need the same reassurance that we all do about about our worth to another person. With a bit of improvisation, satisfactory techniques can be developed within the confines of limited movement or sensation. Different positions can be tried, K-Y jelly used where lubrication is a problem, and incontinence dealt with.

However you choose to experiment, talk to your partner. Ask her how your touching feels, tell her how her touching feels. Sex provides opportunities for communicating on many different levels. Relax and enjoy it.

Sensuality doesn't begin and end in bed, it may start on the dance floor or in the way that your thighs touched in the bus on the way home. But how do you proceed from there? Soft light, soft music and lots of touching and kissing seems to be the general answer. Women are often concerned about cleanliness, so a bath or shower together can not only allay this fear, but can be very sensual in itself. Undressing each other slowly, kissing and caressing each bit as it becomes uncovered – back of her neck, shoulders, arms, breasts and so on – all can be part of the love making process. Candlelit baths with bubbles are not only romantic, but can help with any shyness you may feel.

Remember the bath you had when getting to like yourself? Now you can get to know her. Wash each other, turning each movement into a caress, but do be careful not to use strongly perfumed soaps on genital regions. Don't forget to talk; if you are a bit apprehensive or scared don't be afraid to say so. And when you get out towel each other dry.

I must admit that I have an attraction to water, and I have

included the above only as a suggestion. It may not suit you or your situation, a lukewarm bath in a cold, mouldy, communal bathroom may not have the same appeal. But whatever your circumstances, you can work out an equivalent scenario to suit yourselves.

Touching, caressing, holding and kissing are the four cornerstones in women's lovemaking, and they will help you know where to go next. Women's breasts are often an erogenous zone (those parts of the body that are especially sensitive to touching, kissing and so on); they can be used to heighten arousal. Some women have described what they feel as a 'direct connection' between their breasts and their clitoris. Try finding her other erogenous zones – the back of her neck, the small of her back, behind her knees, her earlobes, her feet. And while she is experimenting with you, you may discover erogenous zones you never knew you had.

Rubbing

Rubbing your bodies together may also be stimulating. You might like to try it in a sort of mirror position with your breasts, stomachs and cunts touching. However, there aren't any rules, and no reason why you shouldn't try it facing in opposite directions or sideways or half-sitting or any way you want as long as it feels good. Hand or body lotion spread between you can help make movement easier.

For some women, the clitoral stimulation gained from rubbing is the most important and fulfilling to them. It might be the way that makes them come (or orgasm); for other women it is only one part in the love making process:

> I didn't think I'd ever have an orgasm. Then one afternoon when we were making love I was lying on her back and rubbing myself against her – I couldn't believe it when I came.

Oral sex

There are lots of terms for oral sex: eating, licking, going down, sixty-nine and so on. It is a common sexual practice between women and basically consists of mouth/genital contact. It is helpful if you feel good about yourself and are at ease with your cunt, and the lubricating juices which it produces. If you haven't tasted your own juices whilst masturbating, try it. Making love with another woman won't taste so different. However, there may be concerns about hygiene and cleanliness because the genitals also encompass the urethra (where urine comes out). If you can have a bath or wash before making love it will probably help you both to feel more relaxed. But beware of douching (washing out the vagina with water or chemicals). It's an unnecessary process as the vagina is self-cleaning – slightly acidic fluids are produced naturally which keep germs in check. If you douche too frequently, you can interfere with this natural cleansing process.

I will describe oral sex from the perspective of the woman who is 'going down.' That doesn't mean that your partner should be completely passive, that the roles can't be reversed, or that you can't both do it at the same time. We will move on to that, but for now we will concentrate on one woman 'going down'.

Remember the four cornerstones of lovemaking – touching, caressing, holding and kissing – they're important here, too. Move down her body slowly, taking care to touch and kiss. Extend your attention down her belly, across her hips and down the tops of her thighs. Then, either using your fingers or tongue or both, gently open up the lips of her cunt. She may well be wet from lubricating juices, but the amount of juice that women produce varies. If she is not very wet you can use your saliva to moisten her lips and clitoris. Now start experimenting, and your partner should react. She may move your head with her hands to guide you, or she may move her body; she may give you verbal directions. There are many things that you can do as variations as she becomes more stimulated. You could try long strokes with your tongue, from her clitoris to her vagina and back again. You could lick the lips of her cunt, suck her clitoris or lick it softly. Using your fingers may also excite her. You may find out what she likes by being 'plugged in' to her responses.

Most women need to have their clitoris stimulated in order to orgasm, but remember: the more stimulation the clitoris receives, the more sensitive it becomes. Direct licking or sucking may become too much, or a bit painful near orgasm. Try different things; use your whole mouth, even talking or groaning creates vibrations that will stimulate her clitoris. Be careful of your teeth, a nick to any part of the cunt can be painful. If she does orgasm (come) there's no harm in licking those juices up as well, but she may find her clitoris sensitive to the slightest touch.

A lot of women feel self-conscious and dirty during their period. This is mainly to do with the way we are brought up. If both of you feel OK about having oral sex when you have a period, then there's nothing wrong with that – it's just a bit messier sometimes. However, if either of you is HIV positive or there is any chance that either of you might be (if either of you are, or have been, injecting drug users, bisexual or partners of people in these groups) you should avoid oral sex during periods. If you are worried about oral sex at other times because one of you is HIV positive, you might consider doing what some American lesbians are doing: using a latex barrier/dental dams.

For oral sex you can either work your way down your partner's body while she lies on her back, until you are lying between her legs or she could kneel above you straddling your face. Or you could try the famous '69' position facing in opposite directions and simultaneously 'eating and being eaten'. Although it is not impossible to have orgasms at the same time, many women report difficulty in concentrating on their own orgasm whilst thinking about the other person's.

As with 'rubbing', some women might find oral sex the most stimulating and satisfying way to enjoy lovemaking whilst others may want to be penetrated before, after or in conjunction with oral sex:

One of my most erotic memories was my girlfriend

'eating' me after a bath together. I started off standing, leaning against the wall, moved to half-sitting on the edge of the bath, and eventually came lying on the bath mat. It was a hot, impulsive and very intense session.

Penetration

Whilst there are those who will say that when lesbians want to be penetrated, what they really want is a man, it's really just another myth. For those who say that the vagina was designed to accommodate a penis, I would suggest that they look at the ends of their hands. We all have fingers, and many women prefer being penetrated by fingers which are sensitive and have more freedom of movement. They can also be used in different multiples and don't go flaccid just when orgasm is imminent.

It is up to you to explore and decide whether you or your partner likes to be stimulated by being penetrated with fingers. Again, penetration may be used in conjunction with any of the above, or other sexual practices.

If you do practise penetration, take off any rings that you wear, and ensure that your nails are short and don't have jagged edges. If you are going to use a lubricant, choose a water-based one (eg. KY jelly.) The oil-based ones like vaseline may lead to infections. If you put your fingers in your partners anus make sure you wash your hands before touching her cunt (or yours) again.

Summary

★ The better you feel about your own body, the better you will feel about making love to another woman.

★ Feeling good about yourself doesn't mean looking like a magazine model, it means acknowledging and liking your uniqueness.

★ Talking with your partner will help you feel relaxed, and help achieve a good relationship both in bed and out of it.

★ There is no right way or wrong way to make love, no set pattern, sequence or timetable.

Common concerns and problems

The main fear most women have about making love with other women is not knowing what to do, or the fear of 'not doing it right'. Hopefully some of those anxieties have been addressed above. Talking, taking your time and relaxing will probably put paid to any initial apprehensions. Be sensitive to any anxieties which your partner is exhibiting. Reassurance will pay dividends.

There are a number of other common concerns about lesbian sex. Many of these are linked with society's attitude towards sex in general, and the way that women are viewed. Women seldom talk about concerns they have about sex and sexual practices; a concern is not necessarily a problem unless one or both of you decide that it is. Lesbians have both similar and different problems to heterosexual women, these include:

★ Not having an orgasm (or coming). If either you or your partner don't have orgasms and would like to achieve them, then there are a number of steps which you can take. Some women are quite happy not to have orgasms, either with a partner or when masturbating, these women are often referred to as 'pre-orgasmic' rather than 'non-orgasmic', because it is often just a matter of time and changing attitudes until they do.

Most women have reported that their first orgasm was reached when masturbating. One of the ways to approach this concern is to experiment with masturbation and to make a note of what techniques turn you on the most, or bring you to orgasm by yourself. Also note which fantasies work most often. You don't necessarily have to tell your partner about these, but it may help to fantasize when she is making love to you. If you are able to come when masturbating, but not with a partner, tell her – or preferably show her – how you manage it. If you use a vibrator remember that this can be used when you make love together too. There is no reason why you should orgasm every time you make love but if you would like to, there's no reason why you can't bring yourself to orgasm by masturbating.

★ Passivity is a concern among lesbians. Some women don't want to make love to their partners and prefer to remain passive. This may reflect the woman's general attitude toward her sexuality ('I'm not really a lesbian because I don't make love to other women.') It may be merely a matter of habit and practise. If a woman has had a previous relationship with someone who didn't let her make love to them, then a pattern may have been built up and confidence eroded.

★ Some women have conflicts about certain parts of their bodies or particular practices like oral sex. Restricted or rigid loving making patterns may be a source of frustration and boredom. The more you can experiment with practices and positions the wider the choice of activities you will have to negotiate around. Naturally nobody should be coerced into doing things they don't want to do. Sex should be mutually satisfying, and lesbian sex has all the potential to be that.

The aversion some women feel to certain sexual practices may be as a result of bad adult experiences or childhood trauma. If a particular sexual activity is associated with rape or incest or other kind of abuse then the woman may want to avoid these because of the unpleasant emotions it arouses. Some women find it difficult to feel good about masturbating because of punishment they may have received when young. These issues are the symptoms of a particular woman's history and the source of concern can be dealt with in therapy. Therapy doesn't carry the same taboos in lesbian communities as it does generally. Lots of women have therapists (usually lesbian therapists) and find them very helpful and positive.

★ Frequency of love making (rather than the quality of it) is another common problem. Once again there are no rules about how often you should make love. However, especially if you are in a monogamous relationship, differing levels of sexual needs may cause tension. If this is happening in your relationship, then acknowledge the problem and try to come up with a compromise. With good will on both sides it is possible to negotiate a happy medium.

Of course, differing levels of sexual need may be a temporary thing connected with stress and anxieties outside of the relationship. There may be a period of unusually heavy physical demands upon one of the partners which leaves her feeling less keen to have sex. Try to be sensitive to each others needs. If this pattern has a discernible cause that is temporary, then be patient. Dealing with a family bereavement or starting a new job will probably leave most of us mentally and physically drained. Some medications can have the same effect. During these times of added stress it's important to be aware of what is happening and not feel personally slighted or responsible.

However, it has to be said that sexual problems often indicate that there is something more fundamentally awry with the relationship. But that is something that only honest discussion will reveal between you.

★ Concerns about lubrication are very common and probably the easiest to deal with. If you find that your cunt juice is sparse or insufficient, buy some water based lubricating jelly (KY jelly is sold in most chemists). You can also incorporate this into your love making. Experiment with different flavoured jellies (you'll probably have to go to a 'marital aids' or sex shop to get these, or order through a catalogue). If you feel that you're positively gushing juices this too can either be towelled up or incorporated into your sexual activities. Remember with most women the amount of vaginal fluid produced varies through the menstrual cycle anyway.

★ Severe pain on penetration is often due to tension. If pain persists despite gentle care and patience, combined with lots of lubrication, then there may be a medical reason for the pain. These could range from vaginal infections to venereal diseases, menopause or scarring during rape or childbirth. In the case of anal penetration, the pain could be caused by haemorrhoids (piles). It is worth consulting your local Well Woman Clinic, G.P. or a gynaecologist if you are concerned.

8: HEALTH

Being happy as a lesbian must include looking after health and well-being. After all, it's unlikely you'll be happy if you're ill. And this doesn't just mean avoiding sexually transmitted diseases, or being physically fit. Being healthy is taking care of our whole selves: our physical health (whatever it may be), our mental health, and our emotional well being. This book doesn't have the scope to address all of these issues in detail, but there are a number of books and organisations which can guide you if you wish to pursue any particular aspect further (see the resources list).

General health issues

As with the general population of women in Britain, the number of lesbians who smoke and/or drink is increasing. Many of the social facilities available to lesbians are based in pubs or nightclubs. There is a focus on alcohol and few, if any, smoke free venues. Even those who choose not to smoke may find that they are exposed to passive smoking (inhaling other people's smoke). There still seems to be an image of relaxation related to having a drink or a cigarette in your hand. Understandably, many lesbians – especially those who are just coming out – try to camouflage their nervousness with these handy props.

Smoking

If you don't smoke don't start. If you do, try to give up or at least cut down. Smoking not only affects your health it will affect the health of other people who have to inhale your second hand fumes. Smoking can damage many aspects of your well being; for example, it may increase your chances of developing cervical cancer by seven times if you smoke 20 a day (other factors are also involved of course.) Heart disease is also closely linked with smoking.

The smell of cigarettes on your breath and in your hair and on your clothes might interfere with your chances of becoming intimate with people you might otherwise feel attracted to – finding Ms Right may be that much less easy if you're addicted to the weed.

Why not have a go at giving up – it's probably the most positive step you can take towards improving your health. Think of the advantages: you'll lose that smokers cough; you'll suffer fewer colds and infections; and you could be richer by £7- £12 a week.

Bear in mind that smoking is a habit which has become closely linked with certain times and places in your life. If you break the links, you can break the habit. Avoid the situations where you are likely to want a cigarette. If you can't avoid them, try very hard to resist the temptation. Replace the old habits with new ones – ones that don't have the smoking connection.

The Health Education Council suggests these tips to help you stop:

★ Get your family and friends to sponsor you to stop.

★ Make a bet with someone that you will stop for so long – say three months.

★ Make an agreement to stop with someone else.

★ Talk to your partner or family and tell them what you are going to do.

Ask them to help by being patient and encouraging.

★ Choose a day on which you re going to give up smoking – and make it a big day in your life.

★ Take it one day at a time.

★ Drink fruit juice for breakfast – the taste is fresh and the acidity will help get rid of the nicotine.

★ Plan a treat for the end of the day as a reward for not smoking – a long, luxurious bath, perhaps, or a food treat.

★ If you have a strong urge to smoke, do something else. Distract yourself and don't just sit there thinking about smoking.

★ Some people find other things to do with their hands – knitting or twiddling keys. Some people chew gum. Some people drink a glass of water when they feel the need for a cigarette.

There are a lot of books, leaflets, aides and courses available for those who are intent on giving up smoking. Make sure you have all the information and knowledge at your disposal so that your chances of success are increased.

Drinking

There is a high incidence of alcoholism among lesbians, and for many of them the problems began when they started to question their sexuality. Many women drink to try and hide from their lesbianism, or to give them courage to say what they feel. So, if you don't drink alcohol, try not to start. There is an argument in favour of moderate, well controlled social drinking, but try and keep this in proportion, and certainly don't use having a drink with friends as an excuse to over-indulge.

If you do drink and find that you are having a drink every day, drinking by yourself or beginning to forget things which happened when you were drunk, you need to examine your drinking habits. The first and most important step in dealing with alcoholism is admitting that you have a drink problem. Having a drink problem doesn't mean that you spend all your time intoxicated, or get the shakes if you don't have a drink – these are the more extreme aspects of alcoholism portrayed by the media. Identifying alcoholism as a problem can be difficult at any stage, but if you think that you have a reason for concern then the sooner you admit it to yourself the better. Alcoholism is a disease and like other diseases, the sooner you can spot the symptoms the sooner you can take action and begin to regain control.

Answer all these questions honestly:

★ Do you drink every day or most days? (Even one glass of wine.)

★ Do you drink when you are on your own?

★ Do you always drink until you are intoxicated?

★ Would you find it difficult to drink soft drinks while others were drinking alcohol?

★ Is alcohol interfering with your work? (Do you still feel drunk in the mornings/suffer from hangovers/drink at lunch-times?)

★ Is alcohol interfering with your relationship? (Do you only feel able to do or say things when you've had a couple of drinks? Are you aggressive or violent with your partner when intoxicated?)

★ Are you drinking more now than a year ago?

★ Have you increased the strength of the drinks you are having – having shorts or combinations more often?

★ Do you reach for the bottle when you have a problem or are depressed?

★ Have you ever driven whilst under the influence?

If your answer to any of the above questions is yes, then take a step back and assess whether or not you really have control of your drinking, or whether it is beginning to control you. Dealing with the problem means acknowledging it first, thereafter you can seek support and advice. Listen to your partner or friends if they are trying to tell you that you have a problem – they can often see more clearly than you that you are developing a habit.

So, given that many people drink 'socially' and will continue to do so, what is a reasonable amount? Experts have agreed that for women 14 'units' a week is within safe limits. A 'unit' is counted as half a pint of standard-strength beer or a standard glass of wine, a measure of spirits or a glass of sherry. You should try not to drink on more than four days a week and don't take more than six units in a single day.

Alcoholics Anonymous and Accept both run women only groups and gay groups, contact your local Lesbian Line or Lesbian and Gay Switchboard about the range of support available.

Drugs

There are a range of drugs which may affect our health. Again, the media has concentrated on the affect of the illegal 'hard' drugs, but problems may range from addiction to prescribed drugs (like tranquillisers), to addiction to the recently publicised 'crack.' There are also a number of 'recreational' drugs, some of which are illegal (like marijuana) and some of which are not (like poppers – amyl nitrate and butyl nitrate.) There is no evidence to suggest that the drugs in this latter category are addictive, but the long term effects, especially of poppers are not known.

A major problem amongst women is the use of tranquillisers like Valium, Librium, Ativan, Mogadon and Dalmane which are prescribed by the doctor. Twice as many women use tranx (as minor tranquillisers are called) than men. Doctors usually prescribe tranx to relieve the symptoms of anxiety or, in slightly higher doses, to make us sleep. Tranquillisers relax the muscles; they all have side-effects, regardless of the dose we take. Common side effects are sleepiness, blurred vision and loss of concentration and co-ordination. This can be particularly dangerous if we operate machinery or drive.

If you want to come off tranquillisers, cut down slowly and find your own pace. Remember, you may not be addicted. A lot of emotions which have been suppressed by the tranx are likely to come to the surface, so be prepared to cry, shake and be angry. Talk about it as much as you can. Take good care of yourself during this time – the withdrawal period may last longer than you think. But remember, the withdrawal symptoms will pass. There are many specialist agencies now which are willing to help you come off. Using their accumulated experience and expertise you can make the break less traumatically. (See resource list)

In general terms, the fewer chemicals we pump into our body the better. Drugs, regardless of their category, don't help us deal with problems or fears. They may make things look rosier for a short time, but in the end we have to deal with reality and sort things out. Working through problems is much healthier than trying to hide from them. Dealing with things immediately may be harder but it makes sense. Difficulties may seem even bigger if you have to face them in the depression which often follows the euphoric drug-induced feelings.

If you are an injecting drug user, be aware of the risks you are taking. Every injection from a dirty or shared needle brings with it a risk for yourself and for other people. It's not just AIDS and HIV, but also hepatitis and many other blood borne diseases. Don't share your gear, or use other people's gear. Policies are changing and the concept of needle exchanges are becoming accepted. Use them for the sake of your own health and the health of others. Also, be responsible in your relationships and let partners know about your habit. If you are an injecting drug user, it may be better to practise safer sex all the time. The best advice is of course to seek help and support and try and kick the habit all together.

Diet

Recently there has been more awareness of the importance to our health of what we eat. Many women are moving towards better balanced diets and vegetarian food. These days it's not just the cholesterol and saturated fats which we need to be aware of, but the additives and preservatives which many processed foods contain. There have also been scares about the levels of bacteria contaminating some foods such as eggs and cheese.

In general cut down on processed and refined foods (eg white sugar), fast foods and take aways, red meat, and food with a high level of saturated (and other) fats. Ensure that you eat plenty of fibre, fruit and vegetables. There is an enormous amount of information about food and diet available at present, so make sure you take it on board.

For lesbians living alone, the problem is finding the enthusiasm to cook balanced meals for one person. It's annoying to go to supermarkets and find things packaged in such a way that single portions are hard to find – corner shops might be a better bet for purchasing small quantities, and street markets are better still.

Constantly relying on hastily grabbed 'snacks' can soon become a way of life. Cooking or storage facilities may also be limited if you are living in a small flat or bedsit, or because of cost. If you don't have a fridge, try to buy fresh food in small quantities just before you'll need it. Standing a bottle of milk in a bowl of cold water will help preserve it for a day or two.

Being properly fed simply means getting enough of each nutrient to maintain health and fitness, and which particular food one chooses among the various sources for each nutrient is less important. Include fresh vegetables in at least one meal a day, and buy yourself one of the excellent 'cooking for one' books.

Exercise

Whatever our physical condition, most of us don't do enough exercise. Indeed, the majority of lesbians seem to get their main exercise dancing the night away at the disco. There are many levels of exercise and many ways of doing it – it doesn't necessarily have to be sporty if you're not that way inclined. Decide what you're interested in and then think about either joining a group which undertakes some activity – swimming, walking, softball, aerobics, Tai chi, fencing, dance – or begin a programme at home. The disadvantage of the latter course is the difficulty of keeping up a regime of repetitive exercise in isolation. You need a lot of will-power and self-discipline to cope with the sheer boredom after a while. You'll have much more chance of success if you join some communal activity which is enjoyable in itself. Of course, exercise is something that should become part of your life, not something you do for a while and then forget about.

The four golden rules of exercise are:

★ Get moving. Use more effort than usual by finding a more active way to do the things you normally do; get off the bus a stop or two earlier than usual, use the stairs at work, take up a new activity.

★ Build up gradually. It takes time to get fit. Work hard enough to make yourself a bit sweaty and out of breath, but not uncomfortably so. Always warm up first with a few gentle bends and stretches.

★ Exercise regularly. It'll take 20 or 30 minutes of exercise two or three times a week for you to get fit and stay fit.

★ Keep it up. You can't store fitness.

Exercise is also good for relieving stress and the fitter you are the better you will feel able to deal with day to day demands. It's amazing how much more stamina you can build up in quite a short time. And a healthy body will be more resistant to minor infections.

Stress

Stress can affect us both mentally and physically, and it is important to recognise and acknowledge the many facets of it that can threaten our well-being. For years tension and stress in men's lives has been recognised as a major health hazard, but the effect it has on women has received less publicity. Stress isn't just about high powered jobs and work, it's also about the tension we feel when we haven't come out or if we're thinking of coming out. The stress involved in relationship break-ups, bereavement, moving house, dealing with bills and debts – all these can have disastrous effects on our general health.

When stress is related to being lesbian, we don't have the same sorts of support systems as heterosexual women or men have. It is less likely that a lesbian will receive the support she needs from family and heterosexual friends when her relationship is on the rocks, or when she is trying to come to terms with her sexuality. One way of helping to minimise stress and to deal with the factors which cause it is to get reassurance from other lesbians. There is no need to think you have to deal with it all by yourself; find other lesbians and talk things through.

Unfortunately there are no magic answers to the events in life which make us unhappy – emotional upheaval, bereavement, money worries – all these things are part of being human and we each have to cope in our own way. But sharing troubles with someone who is sympathetic can be amazingly effective in taking the sting out of it.

It might also be useful to learn a few simple relaxation techniques which you can use when you're feeling particularly tense or anxious. Try these:

★ Sit or lie quietly in as peaceful a place as you can find. Close your eyes. Picture a scene of tranquillity, like waves lapping on a sandy beach, or leaves rustling in a gentle breeze. Breathe slowly and deeply through your nose. Make each out-breath long, soft and steady.

★ Sit or lie quietly in a peaceful place. Clench both fists for about fifteen seconds. Then relax them and feel the tension draining away from your arm muscles. Repeat this twice. Then hunch your shoulders for fifteen seconds, and relax, feeling the tension drain away, Repeat twice. Continue the same routine with jaw-clenching and relaxing. And finally, screw up your eyes tightly and relax them, feeling the tension disappear.

★ Sit or lie in a peaceful place and close your eyes. Repeat over and over to yourself a simple sound, word or phrase. Anything as long as it's simple and easy to repeat. Just concentrate on the repetition so that it fills your mind and banishes anxious thoughts. Let yourself relax into this steady rhythm for five or ten minutes.

To summarise:

★ Talk through your worries with a friend or sympathetic counsellor.

★ Deal with problems as soon as they arise. Letting them stew won't make them go away, and delay often makes them worse.

★ Get professional help if appropriate eg. bereavement counselling, debt management, health advice.

★ There are some excellent audio/video tapes available to help you master relaxation. The more you practice, the easier and more effective it becomes. You might also try yoga or meditation.

★ Try massage, either with a friend/partner or a professional.

★ Try to leave work-related problems behind at the end of the day. Don't invite colleagues to call you at home if they have a problem on your day off.

★ Make time to pursue a hobby or sport. Reading, music, films, TV, are all useful escapist pastimes. Exercise will help you cope.

★ Learn to say no. Perhaps an assertiveness course would be useful if this is a problem.

Bear in mind that stress is a very real factor in determining the state of your whole-being health. Stress is not about being a 'neurotic female', it can have serious effects on you both physically (headaches, backaches, psychosomatic problems), and mentally (depression, loss of concentration, despondency.)

My personal experience of stress will illustrate this. When I was at school I had a relationship with another girl; it was very secretive and we promised each other not to tell anyone else about it. When we broke up two years later, I was devastated. I had to deal with the grief of losing her without anyone to discuss it with. I thought I was coping, but I developed eczema, my migraines increased, and I acquired a twitch. Eventually, I was booked into the hospital to have neurological tests. I had EEGs and pins pricked into my fingers. Apparently my symptoms were in keeping with those of a disease similar to Parkinson's. Yet they couldn't find anything organically wrong. Then the neurologist asked me if there was anything troubling me. I told her the whole story. The effect of unburdening myself was miraculous – most of my symptoms disappeared immediately, and the rest eventually subsided. A simple sharing of my grief had released the tension which had caused my body to react so badly.

Counselling and relaxation should always be considered when personal stress reaches a level which is interfering with your day-to-day functioning.

If conventional medicine is not helping in a particular case, remember that there are alternative therapies, too. Homoeopathy, acupuncture, osteopathy and several other techniques might be worth investigating. These are not generally available on the National Health, but if your conventional doctor can't help, by all means look into these other means of treating illness. You'll find complementary therapists listed in yellow pages. Your local women's centre or lesbian line may also have lists of recommended therapists. If you do decide to try a complimentary practitioner, make sure that she or he is registered with some kind of regulatory body.

9: SEXUALLY TRANSMITTED DISEASES

Lesbians are one of the least vulnerable groups of sexually active people in terms of all sexually transmitted diseases, including AIDS. But we can and do get a variety of other infections and diseases, and we need to be informed about them. Knowledge in this area is important not only for our own health and well being, but the health of our partners.

AIDS

Lesbians are a 'low risk' group for AIDS although you probably wouldn't have known this from coverage of the disease in the media. However, a few lesbians have become infected with HIV (Human Immunodeficiency Virus – the virus which is thought to be responsible for AIDS) by various routes and so we need to safeguard ourselves against possible infection. Knowledge of the virus and the way it is transmitted is, at present, the only protection we have against it.

Activities which carry the highest risk of infection for lesbians can include injection of drugs from shared or dirty needles and syringes or working as a prostitute. Lesbians who are the sexual partners of bi-sexual men, or who have received infected semen during artificial insemination are also vulnerable. There have been no reported cases of HIV transmission attributable directly to lesbian sexual practices. But that doesn't mean we can be complacent about the issue.

AIDS stands for Acquired Immune Deficiency Syndrome; it

is caused by the Human Immunodeficiency Virus (HIV.) There isn't a test which will show whether people have the virus in their body, but there is a test which can show whether the body has manufactured antibody to the virus.

If the test shows that a person is antibody positive (which means they have the antibodies to HIV in their blood) it means that they have been in contact with the virus.

At this stage they may be asymptomatic (showing no symptoms), but could later go on to develop the full syndrome. The virus then attacks the immune system and renders the sufferer open to all kinds of infections and infestations which the body would otherwise fight off without much problem. It is these repeated infections which eventually lead to death. You could think of having AIDS as a bit like fainting in the High Street: you wouldn't die from that, but it would make you vulnerable to being run over by buses or cars or motorcycles; not all of these vehicles (infections) would necessarily kill you, but they would certainly do you harm.

AIDS is not easily transmitted. There is no risk from ordinary social contact – you don't get it from coughs or sneezes or handshakes or lavatory seats. HIV is carried in the blood and through body fluids (including semen, vaginal secretions and menstrual blood). It is a relatively frail virus and dies quickly once outside the body. You can become infected by the virus if the body fluids or blood of an infected person enters your own body through cuts, breaks in the skin or mucosal surfaces (like the vaginal and anal walls). An example of how the virus might be transmitted between two women would be if a woman with cuts on her fingers penetrated the vagina of an infected woman who was having her period. A woman with bleeding gums or mouth ulcers would also be at risk if she practised oral sex on a partner, especially during the infected partner's period.

Find out about your partner's sexual history: has she ever had sexual relationships with partners in the 'high risk groups'? Does she use, or has she in the past used, dirty or shared needles to inject drugs? Has she ever worked as a prostitute? If the answer to all these questions is no, then there should be little reason to worry. If the answer is yes to any of them, then perhaps precautions would be wise until you have had counselling from one of the AIDS organisations who will be able to advise you on the best course of action.

Although this is, at present, a minor problem for lesbians, if you have any doubts at all you should practise safer sex. Guidelines about safer sexual practices are constantly being updated as more is found out about HIV and AIDS. If you are HIV positive, or think you might be because of a high-risk relationship or activity, then contact the telephone helplines for advice and up to date information. It is wise to be careful when dealing with blood from other people, not only because of HIV, but also other blood-borne diseases, such as hepatitis.

Other ways of reducing risk:

★ If you have sex with men, especially vaginal or anal intercourse, make sure that he wears a condom.

★ If you decide to have artificial insemination, screening of the potential donor is imperative. Remember, even someone who has tested negative or who seems healthy, might be carrying the virus. The main agencies who specialise in artificial insemination are now screening donors.

★ If you are in a 'high risk group' or have been diagnosed as having HIV, then avoid becoming pregnant. Pregnancy puts extra strain on the immune system and increases the chances of an infected woman developing AIDS. Babies born to mothers infected with HIV are often themselves infected and may develop full AIDS.

AIDS; if in doubt find out. If you are not sure about something or want reassurance then telephone one of the helplines. Remember worry and stress can also affect your health and produce AIDS-like symptoms. (See resources list)

Other sexually transmitted diseases

If you think you may have a sexually transmitted disease, get medical help as soon as possible. You can visit your local special clinic (genito-urinary clinic) without an appointment – simply turn up. You ll find the address of your nearest clinic listed in the phone book under VD (venereal disease) clinic. Discretion is the keyword in these clinics and you have no need to fear shock or censure; their business is to treat these diseases, not to discourage people from attending by moralising at them.

Crabs (*Phthirus pubis* or crab louse)

These lice are more of a nuisance than a danger and can be dealt with fairly easily with treatments from a chemist which you can buy over the counter. They are generally passed on by close physical contact, but they can survive away from their human host for up to twenty-four hours, so this is one pest you can pick up from a lavatory seat.

Although you can see crabs with the naked eye, you'll probably feel them first: they cause intense itching in the pubic area. You might see them crawling about or you might find nits (eggs) in your pubic hair or underclothes. It's best to deal with them as soon as possible. The adult crab can survive without a human host for over a day, so it's possible to pick them up by sharing bedding or clothes with an infected person. Bear this in mind when you're treating them, and make sure that all your clothes and linen are washed at a high temperature. Unless you want to be reinfected, ensure that your partner(s) and flatmates are also treated. Use only the proper self-treatments you can get from the chemist.

Other lice (body lice and head lice)

Though not necessarily sexually transmitted, they can pass easily between people living in close proximity, especially if there is shared clothing, bedding, combs etc. It is also possible to infect/contract threadworms (pinworms) from sexual contact. Itching of the anus will probably be the first sign. They are easily dealt with, using an ointment available on prescription from your G.P.

Thrush

This is an infection caused by the yeast *Candida Albicans*. There are traces of this yeast in healthy vaginas, but the yeast is kept in check by other bacteria which live there and by the slightly acid environment of your cunt. You may have slight thrush infections regularly which the body deals with without your ever being aware of it. There are lots of reasons why the yeast culture may suddenly thrive, common causes are taking antibiotics, feeling run-down, douching excessively and diabetes. Itching and a slightly creamy discharge are common symptoms, others include a yeasty odour, redness and swelling of the vulva and perhaps pain or burning when urinating.

Thrush is easily diagnosed by a doctor and the treatment is usually a cream or vaginal suppository. Some women treat themselves and swear by natural yoghurt – dip a tampon into the yoghurt and insert it into your vagina. Remember to change the tampon often.

Thrush can be transmitted to sexual partners, for example by sharing a vibrator. It can also be introduced from the rectum into the vagina by improper wiping after a bowel movement. A woman should always wipe herself from the front to the back, never from the rectum towards the vagina.

Though irritating, thrush and other yeast infections aren't considered to be dangerous medical conditions.

Trichomoniasis

Also called trich and TV. This condition is caused by bacteria which (like yeast) are usually present in healthy vaginas. The symptoms are a yellow-green discharge, itching and an inflamed labia. Again this is easily diagnosed and treated by a GP, and does not lead to any dangerous medical condition.

Non-specific vaginitis

'Vaginitis' means an infection of the vagina and 'non-specific' means the doctor has been unable to pinpoint the organism responsible for it. The symptoms are a discharge (sometimes streaked with blood) and redness and itching of the vulva. The bacteria which causes NSV can be dealt with by prescribed vaginal suppositories or cream or maybe oral medication from your doctor. These infections can be passed to your partner (and back again.)

Gonorrhoea

(The clap or a 'dose') is one of the most common sexually transmitted diseases. Gonorrhoea is caused by bacteria and can therefore be easily treated by antibiotics (eg. penicillin). One of the problems with gonorrhoea is that you may be infected and not have any symptoms. It is much easier to test men for gonorrhoea, the test used on women is not as reliable. The problem is that symptoms (described below) may be so mild in women that they go unnoticed. When undetected and untreated gonorrhoea can lead to severe medical problems.

If you do have symptoms, they will show within a week of contact with an infected person. Symptoms may include: vaginal discharge, itchy or uncomfortable urethra (where the urine comes out), you may experience diarrhoea or discomfort before and after bowel movements (like feeling that you need to go to the loo again even though your bowel is empty.)

The bacteria can be passed between women even though it is very frail away from the warm, wet environments in which it thrives. The bacteria can infect the vagina, urethra, anus and mouth and can be passed between these areas. If your partner is infected you may become infected in your mouth by oral sex, or in your vagina or urethra if she used her fingers in her cunt and then in yours.

If one of your sexual partners has been tested positive for gonorrhoea then, even though it is more difficult for women to pass the infection on, get tested. Where our health is concerned it is better to be cautious.

Chlamydia

Has similar symptoms to gonorrhoea, and is treated in much the same way. Women are likely to be asymptomatic (without symptoms) for chlamydia. If left untreated it can lead to other serious conditions like pelvic inflammatory disease and infertility.

Cystitis

Cystitis is an inflammation inside the bladder. Over half the women in Britain suffer from it at some time during their lives, often repeatedly. Although cystitis is very distressing, it is often more of a nuisance than a danger to your health. It is caused either by germs in the bladder or allergies to toiletries – stress can also play a part.

A typical attack of cystitis will consist of one or more of the following symptoms:

★ A burning or scalding pain in the urethra (urine passage) when you pass water.

★ A need to pass water more often than usual. And even though you are bursting to go, there may be hardly any water to pass.

★ A feeling that you are going to lose control of your bladder.

★ A fever or ache in your lower abdomen or back.

★ Cloudy urine or blood in the urine.

There's a lot you can do to relieve an attack of cystitis. Even if it starts at night, it's best not to try and forget about it. The sooner you do something about it, the more chance you have of clearing it up.

1. Immediately drink a pint of water. This will be the first of

many. Drinking a lot of fluid will help flush the germs out of the bladder.

2. If you are in pain, hot water bottles can be very soothing.

3. Mix a teaspoon of bicarbonate of soda with some water and drink it down. Repeat every hour for the next three hours. It makes the urine more acidic and so stops the bacteria multiplying.

4. Take two mild painkillers.

5. Drink another pint of water – and another every 20 minutes until you've flushed the germs out of your system.

To prevent further attacks: drink at least three or four pints of water every day. Pass water when ever you feel the need – don't hang on if you can help it; see the doctor; don't use antiseptics, talcum powder, perfumed soaps or deodorants in the genital area; if you get cystitis after drinking tea or coffee, try and dilute it or avoid it altogether; avoid wearing tight trousers and try to wear cotton pants and tights with a cotton gusset. Man made fibres don't allow your skin to breathe so easily.

Viruses

In addition to the pests (like crabs) and yeasts and bacteria (like thrush and gonorrhoea), there are also viruses which can be sexually transmitted. Viruses cannot be treated by using antibiotics and it is usually up to the body's immune system to deal with them. HIV is an example of a sexually transmitted virus; because it attacks the immune system, which normally deals with invading viruses, it is particularly dangerous. Viruses can be passed to sexual partners, so if you discover that you are infected take steps to avoid giving what you've got to others.

Hepatitis

An example of a sexually transmitted virus. There are two types of Hepatitis: Hepatitis A (or infectious hepatitis) and

Hepatitis B (which is blood-borne like HIV.)

Hepatitis A is usually contracted through infected food or water. The virus has been found in faeces, so anal/oral contact should be avoided. The symptoms may resemble flu, and the infected person may look jaundiced (yellow), the most infectious period is usually before the appearance of such symptoms. If your partner has hepatitis you may consider getting a gamma globulin injection which will increase your resistance. A change in diet – avoiding alcohol – and lots of rest will probably lead to full recovery without any long term effects and you will have future immunity to Hepatitis A.

Hepatitis B is much more serious and may lead to severe liver damage. Hepatitis B is blood borne, like HIV, but much more virulent and infectious – in fact Hepatitis B has been shown to be 100 times more infectious than HIV. Symptoms may be similar to Hepatitis A, or very mild (like a dose of flu). The infected person may become extremely lethargic, there may be a swelling of the liver and pain in the joints. Jaundice may make the skin and eyes yellow. Urine may turn dark brown and stools light and clay-like in colour. For some people, there may be no symptoms at all. However, even after the initial symptoms have disappeared a long period of recuperation may be needed (sometimes six months to a year). There may still be traces of the virus left in the blood, and this will mean that the sufferer may become a carrier of the disease, still capable of infecting others whilst appearing perfectly well.

Both types of hepatitis can be detected by a blood test. There is now an effective vaccine available to protect against Hepatitis B, so if you think you are at risk, ask your doctor to immunise you.

Precautions like those associated with HIV will prevent infection of sexual partners.

Herpes

Herpes is another virus which comes in two forms. Herpes Simplex type 1 causes cold sores on the lips and mouth, and herpes simplex type 2 which causes similar blisters on the genital area. Once the herpes virus has entered your body, there is no cure and the symptoms will probably recur throughout your life.

Herpes is contagious when the blisters are present and also for a short time before and after their appearance. An infected person doesn't have the blisters all the time, but they can last for up to two weeks when they do appear. The virus then retreats deep into the body until next time the circumstances are right for it to surface, and the blisters heal.

Herpes is contracted when there is contact with the sores; the virus may be carried from one woman to another by fingers, and there may be a cross over of types – a woman with cold sores on her mouth infecting the genital area of someone with whom she is having oral sex.

The symptoms of Type 2 (genital herpes) are: a stinging, tingling or itching in the genital or anal area; flu-like symptoms such as headache, back ache or a temperature; small blisters form, burst and then leave small red ulcers which can be painful. They usually heal within a week or two. Blisters are not always visible; in women they may be inside the vagina or on the cervix. The first outbreak is usually the most severe, but the herpes may never recur again. However, for some people the symptoms may return when they're fatigued or tense, they can also be triggered by over-exposure to the sun.

The Health Education Council gives the following advice to help relieve the symptoms during an attack:
1. Get medication from your doctor. It can be very effective when started early, although it is not a cure.
2. Bathe the infected area in a salt solution: a heaped teaspoonful of salt to a pint of tepid water. Do this for five to ten minutes, two to four times daily.
3. Take an aspirin or other mild painkiller if the pain is severe.
4. If the pain is still severe, try applying an ice pack to the sores.
5. If passing urine is painful, do it in a warm bath.
6. Avoid hot baths if they make the pain worse.
7. A cool shower may help soothe the sores.

8. If it's practical, leave the sores exposed to the air as much as possible to avoid irritation from clothing and to help the sores dry out.

9. Avoid sunbathing and don't use sunbeds, as these make the sores more painful.

10. Keep the sores dry. Dabbing on a little witch hazel – available from your chemist – can help dry out the sores.

The blisters and sores are highly contagious and the virus can be passed on to others through contact, so avoid any direct contact between the sores and other people. These are steps you can take to avoid passing the virus to others:

★ No kissing when you or your partner has cold sores around the mouth.

★ No oral sex when you or your partner has cold sores or genital herpes.

★ No genital contact when you or your partner has genital herpes.

★ Always wash your hands with soap and water after touching the sores.

★ Don't share towels and face flannels.

★ Never use saliva to wet contact lenses.

Genital herpes is serious because there is no cure and because having the disease increases a woman's chance's of getting pre-cancerous and cancerous conditions of the cervix. Women suffering from genital herpes must have regular smear tests.

Genital warts

These are caused by a virus similar to the virus which causes external warts. There is growing evidence that the presence of the genital wart virus (which seems to be aided by smoking and the presence of the herpes virus) contributes to the growth of abnormal cervical cells and cervical cancer. This virus is often passed on from a male sexual partner. Lesbians and nuns are almost completely exempt from this infection IF they have never slept with a man. The wart virus can be identified by smears (PAP tests) and cervicography (where a photograph is taken of the cervix).

Treatment is by means of a special solution which is painted on the warts causing them to fall off, or by means of laser therapy the latter has a 97% probability of complete cure.

Syphilis

Syphilis is caused neither by bacteria or by viruses, but by a spirochaete which is a separate class of organism. The syphilis spirochaete is like a little corkscrew and it can enter the body through the skin. Although this usually happens in moist warm genital areas of sexual contact, it can occasionally enter other areas like fingers or lips.

At the point that the spirochaete enters, the skin becomes swollen. About 3-4 weeks after the spirochaete has entered the body (occasionally as little as 10 days, or as much as 3 months), a small painless sore or blister called a chancre appears on point of entry. For many women this may be inside the vagina. This first sign often goes unnoticed by infected women, even if it is somewhere more visible. Although you will be infectious during this 'primary stage' a blood test for syphilis will not show up positive.

After a period of one to eight weeks the chancre will disappear. You will now enter the 'secondary stage'. You will be highly infectious throughout this stage although you may have no symptoms. On the other hand you may have a rash or develop syphilitic warts which are large and fleshy and usually occur on the genitals. This stage will be over in two weeks or so, and thereafter the spirochaete will enter a latent stage – it will go into hiding. During the latent stage syphilis will show up in a blood test but you won't be infectious. However syphilis may be passed on to an unborn child.

For many the spirochaetes may never emerge from the latent period, but for others after some time – it could be decades – the disease makes its final appearance in what is called the tertiary stage. It can then attack the brain, spinal column and other organs causing permanent damage. The disease can be halted in its progress by antibiotics. If left untreated it may kill or disable the infected person.

Syphilis is far less common than it used to be, but if you have cause to worry about it (eg. you are contacted by a past lover who has had a positive test) make sure that you get checked out. Treatment is, like gonorrhoea, a large dose of penicillin (or similar antibiotic).

Detection and diagnosis of STD's

If you are sexually active, especially if you have a number of partners, it is sensible to have a check-up fairly regularly. This is probably easiest at your local STD clinic, but you can see your local GP. Remember it's not just your health at risk, but that of partners as well. Internal examinations, smear tests and swabs should detect any infection which you may have picked up. But remember that syphilis is usually only diagnosable through blood tests, so if you have cause to worry on that score then request a blood test.

Smears or PAP tests (short for Papanicolaou smear) are not completely reliable, and about 50% of the time report a false negative (i.e. report that there are no abnormalities when in fact there are.) If you are sexually active, especially if you have slept with men in the past, you should have a smear test regularly, at least every three years but preferably more often. Frequent tests can compensate to some extent for their unreliability. Abnormal cells can be easily destroyed by laser treatment which has a 97% probability of complete cure. Naturally, the sooner such conditions are identified the easier they are to deal with.

To have a smear test you will need to remove all of your lower garments and lay on a table. The doctor will then insert an instrument called a speculum into your vagina. This pushes the walls of the vagina apart so that the doctor can clearly see your cervix – it might be uncomfortable, but it doesn't hurt. The doctor then collects some cells from your cervix on a small spatula and sends them off to a laboratory for testing under a microscope.

116

About 2,000 women die from cervical cancer each year. Most of them could have been saved if they'd taken regular smear tests to reveal the condition at an earlier stage.

Summary

The infections and diseases mentioned above are ones which sexually active people might contract. The great news is that as a lesbian you are far less likely to get infected by sexually transmitted diseases than heterosexual people or gay men. All the same, knowing the facts is a good way to ensure that you know what to do if you should encounter any of the ailments I've listed. Being sexually active means that we have to take some responsibility for our health and the health of our partners, it is better to take precautions than risks.

If you have any doubts about your health, or think you may have come into contact with any of these diseases, seek medical help immediately. As we have discovered, many of them can lurk in the body without our realising it, and can cause serious problems later. If you discover that you do have any of these conditions, it is your duty to tell any subsequent partners you may have had, so that they can take steps to protect their own health.

10: THE LAW

British law doesn't recognise lesbians and, contrary to popular belief, doesn't legislate against gay men either. What is contained in the statutes relates only to sexual acts, not to sexual orientation. The first time the word 'homosexuality' was included in the law was in 1988 when the now infamous Section 28 of the Local Government Bill (or as it is now formally known, 2A of the Local Government Act 1986) came into effect.

Having said that, there are many ways in which the law discriminates against lesbians (and gay men) and, unlike some other countries, there is no protective legislation outlawing discrimination against an individual because of their sexual orientation. The general situation is summarised by Paul Crane in his book *Gays and the Law* (Pluto Press, 1982):

> The law as it affects gay men and lesbians in Great Britain reflects and reinforces popular prejudices about us and attempts to place various limitations on the development of our lives as openly gay people. The law affects our sexual and emotional development, our relationships, our leisure, where we work, what we read, whether we can be parents and keep our children, the exercise of our civil rights and how far we can support and help ourselves.[1]

1. *Gays and the Law* by Paul Crane (Pluto Press, 1982)

Sexual relationships

It is illegal for any woman under the age of sixteen to give consent to sexual relationships with either women or men. If your partner is under sixteen (even if you are only one year older) you could be prosecuted for indecent assault, although prosecutions are rare. For young lesbians the intervention of Local Authority Social Services Departments is more likely. Social Workers have the power to apply to the courts to have a young lesbian put into care if it can be established that she was exposed to 'moral danger'. It is not unknown for disapproving parents to initiate these proceedings if they discover that their daughter is having a lesbian relationship:

> My mother was very shocked when she found out about our relationship. She called me a lot of unpleasant things and had me put into care.(Young Lesbian, Aged 17)

Sex between women of any age is specifically prohibited in the armed forces; 'offenders' can be court martialled and sent to prison. This prohibition includes having a sexual relationship with a civilian whilst not on active service. Members of the armed forces who are suspected of being lesbians can be legitimately discharged from the forces.

These are the laws which relate specifically to lesbian relationships. There are of course a number of laws which are used in a discriminatory way against lesbians. For instance, 'outraging public decency' (Section 5 of the Public Order Act) has been used to charge two women who were kissing 'in public' after a march, even though the police received no complaints from 'the public'.

The police

If you are arrested by the police, don't expect them to be sympathetic. You should, however, co-operate with them to the extent of giving your name and address and going to the police station with them. You have the right to know if you have been arrested and on what charge. You have the right not to give them any more information than your name and address until you have had legal advice. Don't be taken in by any promises – the police don't have any power to keep your name out of the papers if you plead guilty. And resist the temptations to plead guilty just to get the whole thing over with; there are long term implications – not least of which is having a criminal record and having to declare any convictions when you apply for jobs, etc.

If you are stopped by police:

★ Stay calm and be polite – don't try to run away.

★ Give your name and address if asked to do so.

★ Ask why you have been stopped.

★ Be careful about answering any questions.

★ If in doubt, politely refuse to answer questions until you have obtained legal advice.

★ Note the officers' numbers all through your contact with them.

★ You can volunteer to go to the police station, but you cannot be detained there without being arrested.

★ If you are detained you will be searched and your possessions listed. Ask to keep your watch, pen and paper so that you can make a record of your detention. Your rights are detailed in the Police Codes of Practice, and you have the right to consult this throughout your detention. Use this right.

★ The police may intimately search you (ie mouth, nose, vagina, anus) for 'Class A' drugs or dangerous items using 'reasonable force.' However, the police cannot take 'intimate body samples' (eg blood) without your written consent. The samples should be taken by a doctor or nurse.

★ Finger prints and photographs may be taken without your consent.

★ Afterwards (and throughout if you have paper and pen) write down everything that has happened including the times. Sign and date the notes, they may be useful as evidence or if you wish to make a complaint about the way in which you have been treated.

If you are arrested you can contact a sympathetic solicitor through your local lesbian or gay switchboard. It may be worth contacting the specialist lesbian and gay police monitoring groups to let them know why and how you were arrested. (see resources list)

Discrimination

In general terms it is the way that laws are interpreted and the prejudice of the courts and judiciary that has most affect on the lives of lesbians in this country. This negative attitude, and the fact that there are no laws to prevent discrimination, means that lesbians are usually seen as unequal in the eyes of the law.

Employment

Lesbians may be victims of discrimination at work and have no recourse through legislation or tribunals. There are no laws to prevent employers sacking someone simply because they are lesbian, nor is there a law to prevent harassment at work directed against lesbians.

However, there are employment protection laws with general application and laws which aim to prevent discrimination on grounds of race and gender. We need to be familiar with these so that we can use them to our advantage if we are treated unfairly. These rights are discussed in the employment section of this book.

Until such time as there is anti-discrimination legislation which applies to lesbians, we must depend on the Equal Opportunities policies of individual organisations. There is a possibility that these will provide some protection under contract law. Many local authorities include lesbians (or sexuality or sexual orientation) in their Equal Opportunities policies. Some Trades Unions have developed policies to take on the issues of lesbians, and promise (in theory) to protect the rights of their lesbian members should they be discriminated against on the grounds of their sexuality.

Immigration

There is no recognition of, nor provision for, lesbians in British immigration law. The immigration law is generally acknowledged to discriminate against black and ethnic minority people, women and lesbians (and gay men). If you or your partner is here on a temporary basis (either as a student or visitor), then you need to be realistic about your chances of setting up home together permanently in this country. To be honest, very few people qualify to enter Britain for settlement these days, it is usually only possible if they have family here. It is by no means automatic.

One of the groups which may apply for settlement here are refugees. The definition of refugee does not include women escaping violence due to their sex or sexuality. Therefore women fleeing male violence or persecution because of their lesbianism would have to rely on the 'compassion of the Home Secretary', who has an extraordinary amount of discretion.

The Home Secretary's 'compassion' has not yet been seen to include consideration of lesbian couples in the arena of immigration. A recently publicised case illustrates this. An Australian woman in Britain on a two year work permit, fell in love and set up home with a woman from this country. They have had a stable relationship for a number of years, and have recently had a baby (the Australian being the biological mother). Despite all of these factors, and having gone through all the avenues open to them in terms of appealing against the deportation order, the Home Office still seemed intent on deporting the Australian and at the time of writing were merely waiting for her baby to be old enough to travel by air. Although there is ministerial discretion in exceptional circumstances, the break-up of a relationship and family does not seem exceptional enough for them. The couple are at present applying to the European Court of Human Rights to try and have the Home Office decision overturned.

The above example illustrates the case that even if your child/children are British citizens, and you are served with a deportation order, you may not be able to stay in the UK as a result of their citizenship. So children who are British citizens may have to leave the country if they want to stay with their mother.

If here on a temporary basis there are a number of issues which you need to be aware of. Although someone here on a temporary permit may be entitled to 'recourse to public funds' (i.e. claiming income support or Housing benefit), be warned that when you apply to renew your stay this may be refused by the Home Office. Getting benefits now may result in deportation later. Seek specialist advice before you take any steps. (see resources list)

If you get arrested and charged with an 'imprisonable offence', then the court can recommend that you are deported, even if you are not sent to prison. Even if the court doesn't decide to make this recommendation, the Home Office could still deport you on the grounds that your presence is 'not conducive to the public good'. If you are British and your partner doesn't have residency (or vice versa), you may have to look further afield if you want to stay together. For example, a woman with EEC citizenship may settle with her partner in Holland if certain conditions are met. There are a few other countries throughout the world who have a positive approach to lesbian relationships.

Housing

Lesbians may face discrimination in the private sector housing market. Again, in order to protect ourselves we need to know our general rights as tenants. Citizens' Advice Bureaux, law centres and lesbian and gay switchboards may be able to give you specific advice on these issues. The latter may also operate a flat share/accommodation service through which you can find a lesbian flat share.

Buying a flat or house is becoming increasingly expensive

but, if you can afford it, this is a choice which is open to you – either alone, with a partner, or with friends (up to a legal maximum limit of 4 co-buyers). Until recently it was one of the perks of being a lesbian couple, rather than a married couple, to get double mortgage tax relief on one property. However, this has now changed so that mortgage relief is applicable to the property rather than the purchasers. As we've already discussed in the chapter on relationships, making a will is essential if you are undertaking this sort of purchase. If you are buying a house with others it is important that those concerned draw up a contract between themselves in case things go wrong. This agreement should cover such eventualities as one person buying the other person out and agreeing a time period for negotiation.

Although it has become more difficult for two men to buy a property together (because of AIDS and the difficulty of getting insurance), this has not yet affected women to any great degree and income will still be the deciding factor. Do shop around to find the best rates and arrangements – attitudes can differ not only between building societies but also between branches of the same society.

Some local authorities make their council housing available to lesbians and offer joint tenancies to lesbian couples. If you live in a council house or flat it may be worth finding out what the policy of the council is. It might be possible to change a sole tenancy to a joint tenancy if your partner is living with you. This will mean that you will both have security should one partner die, or should the relationship break-up. In the case of Harrogate Borough Council v Simpson (1984), which went to the European Court, it was ruled that a woman who had lived with her lesbian lover in a Council flat for 20 years could not succeed (take over) the tenancy as she had never had her name on the original tenancy agreement and was not a member of her deceased lover's family. She was evicted.

If you know that the local authority to which you are applying has a positive attitude towards housing lesbians then think about making it clear that you are a couple when you apply. This will mean that you will be considered for single bedroom accommodation rather than two-bedroomed accommodation which is usually more scarce.

Many young lesbians find themselves homeless after being thrown out of their parents' home because of their sexuality. If you are under 18 it may be worth contacting your local Council under part III of the Housing Act 1985, on the grounds that you are vulnerable and at risk of sexual or financial exploitation.

Custody

This is another area where lesbians face unfair discrimination and injustice. If you are a lesbian mother who has children from a relationship with a man, you may find yourself in a custody dispute. If there is a dispute about custody the courts will decide which parent gets custody on the basis of 'welfare' and 'the best interests of the child/children'. Unlike custody disputes between heterosexual parents where the mother is granted custody (except in exceptional circumstances), lesbian mothers may lose custody of their children solely because of their sexuality.

If you are a lesbian mother who has children from a heterosexual relationship, it is best to get specialist advice at the earliest possible time. Telephone the Lesbian Custody Project for immediate advice and information about sympathetic solicitors. There are also a number of leaflets and books available. (see resources list)

Parenting

It is possible for single women (including lesbians) to adopt children. It is not possible for any unmarried couple to adopt a child. A court order is necessary for adoption, and the same sort of prejudice which lesbian mothers face may come into play when a lesbian applies for adoption. Again, the 'child's best interests' is the major factor and many judges are still blatantly prejudiced. The sexuality of the woman is seen as more important than her parenting skills and her commitment. However, adoption by lesbians is not totally unknown.

Custodianship

Under the Children Act 1975 there are provisions for 'Custodianship'. These came into force at the end of 1985. Although not designed to allow lesbian couples to acquire legal rights over non-biological children, this provision has made it possible to do so under the Act. The only person who cannot apply for a custodianship order is the child's biological parents. Individuals, including unmarried couples, have the right to apply for the legal custody of a child if that child has been living with them for a certain period of time (at least 12 months if the applicant is not a relative). This is not as final as an adoption order, but it does allow the partner of a lesbian who has a child, and who has been living in their household for some time, to legally gain parental rights should the lesbian mother become seriously ill or die. A lesbian couple may similarly apply for custodianship if they have been sharing a home with a child who is a relative and something untoward happens to the biological parent(s).

Guardianship

Lesbian mothers with children may make provisions in their wills to have their partners named as guardians of their children. This is also applicable when only one partner is the legal adoptive parent.

Making a will

As we have seen from the instances above, the legal system discriminates against lesbians and frequently does not acknowledge the existence or validity of their relationships – however stable and long term they may be. Members of a woman's family (even if she doesn't get on with them or has broken off contact) are seen to have more right than her partner to access and to her estate. We need to be strong enough to insist that we can name our own next of kin if we go into hospital, and we need to make clear our wishes should we die.

Wills are especially important if you are a mother and/or have bought something of value with your partner. You need to make clear who gets what, who will deal with your estate and your funeral arrangements. You will want to name guardians for your children. There are technical rules which need to be followed so it's worth getting advice and guidance.

If you are going to use a solicitor, do phone around for quotes. It might be worthwhile in the first instance to get in touch with groups/helplines to get copies of leaflets and other information. The Gay Bereavement Group offer a will form which you can do yourself, but it is better to have it done professionally to avoid the many pitfalls and potential misunderstandings.

SECTION 28:(2A of the Local Government Act 1986)

The implementation of this piece of legislation brought more debate on the subject of homosexuality and civil rights in general, than any other event of recent years. Its stated purpose is to prevent local authorities 'promoting homosexuality'. The section says:

> (1) A local authority shall not –
> (a) intentionally promote homosexuality or publish material with the intention of promoting homosexuality;
> (b) promote the teaching in any maintained school of acceptability of homosexuality as a pretended family relationship;
> (2) Nothing in subsection 1. above shall be taken to prohibit the doing of anything for the purpose of treating or preventing the spread of disease.

At the time of writing, there have been no cases brought before a court, and therefore no case law to clarify this badly drafted piece of legislation. However, a number of eminent legal experts have given their opinion about the Section and its powers.

The section only covers what local authorities decide to do as corporate bodies. Individuals (eg. employees) cannot be prosecuted under this section. Despite early fears, this legislation will have no effect on general anti-discrimination policies of local authorities. Local authorities may continue to develop and implement anti-discrimination policies in terms of both employment and delivery of services. They will only fall foul of the law if they treat 'homosexuals' in a preferential way which implies that homosexuality is better than heterosexuality, and thereby 'encourage' people to become homosexual. Equality is not the issue, and strategies aimed at achieving equality may continue.

> 'The Government is against discrimination of any form...as ratepayers and electors they (homosexuals) are entitled to receive Council services on the same basis as everyone else. There is nothing in the clause that would damage this right, and allegations to that effect are quite without foundation.' (Margaret Thatcher, Prime Minister in a letter dated 3rd March, 1988)

Lesbian and gay groups can (and do) still get grants from local authorities. In terms of education, local authorities have a limited role in the sex education curriculum, the responsibility for this continues to rest with the school governing bodies. It is important, therefore, that as many lesbians as possible become members of school governing bodies.

The Section does not preclude teachers from dealing in an honest and objective way with homosexuality with pupils in the classroom. It does not require teachers to act contrary to the welfare of their individual pupils,and teachers retain the freedom to counsel pupils who seek advice about their homosexuality/lesbianism. A local authority would not be required to discipline teachers who deal with questions of sexuality and prejudice in ways which they believe to be honest and objective. (This includes a lesbian teacher being honest about their own sexuality.)

The main power of this piece of retrograde and discriminatory legislation is to frighten local authorities into thinking that they cannot undertake positive and specific anti-discrimination work on lesbian (and gay) issues. Self censorship by local authority officers and politicians because of misunderstandings will be the greatest effect of this section.

Although this piece of legislation was very much a step backwards, it had a number of very positive spin-offs. It not only brought the subject of discrimination against lesbians and gay men right to the front of the political arena, it made many local authorities and political parties even more determined to campaign for equal treatment for lesbians and gay men. Lesbians themselves mounted an enormously effective campaign as the legislation passed through Parliament. It politicised many lesbians who were otherwise uninterested, and drew the gay community closer together.

Despite the intentions of the sponsors of this legislation to interfere with the progress being made by lesbians (and gay men), it only succeeded in making us stronger and more determined.

CONCLUSION

This book is designed to serve as a kind of introductory survival guide. It doesn't have all the answers, it doesn't cover all the issues, but hopefully it goes some way to identifying stumbling blocks, and suggesting some practical ways of dealing with them.

I am aware that some chapters may sound like a catalogue of problems and seem a bit depressing. Overall, BEING LESBIAN is not like that. Most women face few, if any, of the problems illustrated but all women will be able to identify with them. The more information we have, the more we know about our rights and where to find advice and support, the smoother our *coming out* journey, and the easier it is to be out.

BEING LESBIAN is not necessarily an easy route, but deciding to live your life positively is something you'll never regret.

Lorraine Trenchard

BIBLIOGRAPHY

Allport G. *The Nature of Prejudice* (Doubleday, 1958)

Califia P. *Sapphistry: The book of Lesbian Sexuality* (Naiad Press Inc, 1980)

Campling J. *Better Lives for Disabled Women* (Virago, 1979)

Crane P. *Gays and The Law* (Pluto Press, 1982)

Curb R. and Manahan N. *Breaking Silence: Lesbian Nuns on Convent Sexuality* (Columbus Books, 1985)

Damien Martin A. *Learning to hide: The Socialisation of the Gay Adolescent* in *Adolescent Psychiatry* Developmental and Clinical Studies Vol.X. (The University of Chicago, 1982)

Greater London Council Equal Opportunities Group: *Challenging Heterosexism in the Workplace* (GLC, 1986)

Greater London Council in co-operation with the Gay Working Party. *Changing the World* (GLC, 1985)

Greater London Council Women's Commitee. *Challenging Heterosexism* (GLC, 1986)

Kinsey et al. *Sexual Behaviour in the Human Female* (W.B.Saunders Co, 1953)

Patton C. and Kelly J. *Making it: A Women's guide to sex in the Age of AIDS* (Firebrand Books, 1987)

Rights of Women Lesbian Custody Group: *Lesbian Mother's Legal Handbook* (The Women's Press, 1986)

Sanderson T. *How to be a Happy Homosexual* (GMP, 1989)

Skeates J. and Jabri D. *Fostering and Adoption by Lesbians and Gay Men* (London Strategic Policy Unit, 1988)

Trenchard L. (Ed) *Talking about young lesbians* (London Gay Teenage Group, 1984)

Trenchard L. and Warren H. *Something To Tell You* (London Gay Teenage Group, 1984)

Vida G. *Our Right to Love: A Lesbian Resource Book* (Prentice Hall Inc, 1978)

Weeks J. *Sexuality* (Tavistock Publications Ltd, 1986)

RESOURCES AND CONTACTS

Many of the groups and organisations have an address that begins with BM followed by a number or name. The BM stands for British Monomarks, an organisation which operates an accommodation address service. It's like a box number which the post office may allocate.

Lesbian lines and Gay Switchboards:

Below are some contact numbers and/or addresses, they will be able to give you more information about your nearest lesbian line or about groups and organisations in your area, or see Gay Times for a comprehensive listing of every gay/lesbian switchboard in the country.

London Lesbian Line
(Mon-Fri 2pm-10pm, Tues-Thurs 7.3Opm-10pm)
01 251 6911
London Lesbian and Gay Switchboard
(24 hours every day)
01 837 7324

Edinburgh Lesbian Line
(Mon and Thurs 7.3Opm-10pm)
031 557 0751
Edinburgh Gay Switchboard
(Mon-Sat. 7.3Opm-10pm)
031 556 4049

Belfast Lesbian Line
(Thurs 7.30-10pm)
0232 238668
Belfast Cara-Friend
(Mon-Weds. 7.30-10pm)
0232 322023

Other Contacts:

Black Lesbian and Gay Centre Project
(Thurs. 6pm-9pm)
01 885 3543

Jewish Lesbian and Gay Helpline
(Mon and Thur 7pm-10pm)
01 706 3123

Lesbian Mothers Custody Project
01 251 6576

GEMMA (for lesbians with/without disabilities),
BM Box 5700,Lodon WC1N 3XX

Catholic Lesbian Sisterhood
BM Reconciliation. London WC1N 3XX.

Lesbian and Gay Christian Movement.
BM 6914. London WC1N 3XX.

Black Lesbian and Gay People of Faith (BLAGPOF)
BM 4390. London WC1N 3XX.

Bookshops:

Gay's The Word Bookshop, 66 Marchmont St. London WC1
01 278 7654

Silver Moon Women's Bookshop, 68 Charing Cross Road, London WC2H OBB.
01 836 7906

Sisterwrite Bookshop, 190 Upper Street,London,N1.
01 266 9782

Feminist Audio Books (FAB), 52-54 Featherstone Street, London EC1 8RT.
01 251 0713

Grassroots Books, 1 Newton Street, Piccadilly, Manchester M1 1HW.
061 236 3112

West & Wilde Bookshop, 25a Dundas Street, Edinburgh EH3
031 556 0079

'Women's Tapeover Quarterly' (Taped digest of feminist publications from all over the world) 66, Oakfield Road, London N4.
01-802 8981.

Coming Out:

Lesbian Lines/gay switchboards : See above

Young Lesbian Groups; these are being set up in most major centres, telephone your local help line for information.

Parents:
Parents Enquiry (advice and support for parents)
Rose Robertson – 01 698 1815

Parents and friends of Lesbians and gays
01 523 2910
(10am-10pm)

Lesbian Mothers:
Lesbian Mothers Custody Project
01 251 6576

Useful reading:

Lesbian Mothers' Legal Handbook, Rights of Women Lesbian Custody Group (The Women's Press, 1986)
Are You Still My Mother? Are You Still My Family? Gloria Guss Back (Warner Books, 1985)
Talking about Young Lesbians. Ed. Lorraine Trenchard (London Gay Teenage Group, 1984)
Something to Tell You, Lorraine Trenchard and Hugh Warren (London Gay Teenage Group, 1984)

Work/Employment:

Lesbian Employment Rights, Room 203, Southbank House, Black Prince Road, London SE1 7SJ.
01 587 1636
Lesbian and Gay Employment Rights (LAGER) as above
01 587 1643

Lifestyles and relationships:

Lesbian Lines/Gay Switchboards (see above)
Lebian Mothers Custody Project (see above)
Gay Bereavement Group: (01 455 8894)

Useful reading:

The New Our Bodies, Ourselves Boston's Women's Health Collective, (Simon and Schuster, Inc. 1984)
Our Right to Love: A Lesbian Resource Book Ed. Ginny Vida,(Prentice-Hall, Inc. 1978)
This Bridge Called My Back: Writings by Radical Women of Colour Eds. Cherrie Moraga and Gloria Anzulda, (Kitchen Table/Women of Colour Press, New York. 1981)
Out for Ourselves: the lives of Irish lesbians and gay men Ed. the Dublin Lesbian and Gay Collective, (Women's Community Press 1986)
Nice Jewish girls: a lesbian anthology Ed. Evelyn Torton Beck, (Persephone 1982)
Rocking the cradle: Lesbian mothers, a Challenge in Family Living Gillian Hanscombe and Jackie Forster, (Sheba 1982)

Sex and Sensuality:

Lesbian Sex Jo Ann Loulan, (Spinsters/Aunt Lute, San Francisco, 1984)
Sapphistry: The Book of Lesbian Sexuality Pat Califia, (Naiad Press Inc. 1980)
Serious Pleasure: Lesbian Erotic Stories by the Sheba Collective, (Sheba, 1989)
Macho Sluts: Erotic Fiction Pat Califia, (Alyson, 1988)
(Note – some of these were written before the advent of AIDS and HIV.)

Health:

Alcoholics Anonymous (AA): (London Information Service) 01 843 8202
Lesbian AA c/o London Friend, 86,Caledonian Road. London N1
01-837 3337

ACCEPT. 200 Segrave Road. London SW6
01-381 3155

Women's Alcohol Centre. 254 St Paul's Road, London N1.
01-226 4581

DAWN (Drugs, Alcohol, Women, Nationally) 39-41 North
Road, London N7 9DP
01 700 4653

Women's Health and Reproductive Rights Information
Centre, 52-54 Featherstone Street, London EC1Y 8RT
01 251 6332

Women's Health Helpline
01 495 4995 .

The Women's Natural Health Centre. 169 Malden Road,
London NW5 4HA
01 267 5301

The Terence Higgins Trust (advice for people with AIDS and
related conditions)
01 242 1010

Positively Women (support group for women who have
AIDS/ARC/HIV) c/o CLASH, Soho Women's Hospital, Soho
Square, London W1
01 734 1794
Herpes Association, 41 North Road, London N7 9PD
01 700 4653

Useful reading:

A Woman in Your own Right - Assertiveness and You Anne
Dickson (Quartet Books 1982,)
Trouble with Tranquillisers (From: Tranx Release, 106
Welstead Avenue, Aspley, Nottingham NG8 5WS Tel: 0602
760550)

The Law:

Lesbian Mothers Custody Project : see above
Lesbian Employment Rights : see above
Gay Bereavement Group : see above
Gay Legal Advice : 01 253 2043
(Nightly 7pm-10pm)
Lesbian and Gay Immigration Group:
BM Welcome. London WC1N 3XX.
Liberty (National Council for Civil Liberties) : 01 403 3888
21, Tabard Street, London SE1

Also Lesbian Lines and Gay Switchboards : see above

Magazines and Newspapers:

The Pink Paper
42 Colebrooke Row,
London N1 8AF
Tel: 01-226 8905
National lesbian and gay newspaper available free each
week from gay pubs, clubs and other outlets. Subscriptions
from the above address.

Capital Gay,
38 Mount Pleasant,
London WC1X 0AP
Tel: 01-278 3764
Freesheet available each week from gay pubs, clubs and
other outlets in the London area. Subscriptions available
from: GCODS, PO Box 44, Welwyn Garden City, AL7 2DE.
Mainly male-orientated.

Gay Times,
283 Camden High Street,
London NW1 7BX
Tel: 01-267 0021
Monthly magazine, mainly of interest to gay men but with some lesbian content. Comprehensive national gay guide.

Square Peg,
BM Square Peg,
London WC1N 3XX
Tel: 01-226 1583
Alternative arts based magazine, run by a co-operative. This quarterly includes challenging graphics, photography and always a varied contents page, increasingly geared to the lesbian reader.

Lesbian and Gay Socialist,
PO Box 83,
Southall,
Middlesex UB1 1QR
Informative and educational quarterly, concerning itself with social issues and current affairs, although good arts coverage as well. Identifies the importance of the gay and lesbian movement to the political left.

Titles of lesbian interest, from GMP

Michael Baker
OUR THREE SELVES: A life of Radclyffe Hall
Radclyffe Hall remains today the most famous of British Lesbians - above all for her novel The Well of Loneliness, which was banned as 'obscene' in a sensational court case in 1928. Her life story, however, is less well known, though she was a leading figure in the colourful homosexual subculture of the 1920s and 30s, and widely connected in the literary world. This comprehensive biography draws upon such unpublished material as letters, diaries and essays, as well as on her novels and poems. Baker throws fresh light on this remarkable woman, and on her two major love affairs with Mabel Batten and Una Troubridge, who together with Radclyffe Hall made up the 'three selves' of the title.
ISBN 0-85449-042-6 £6.95

Michael Elliman and Frederick Roll
THE PINK PLAQUE GUIDE TO LONDON
Lovers of London have always wanted to know where the famous and infamous lived. Blue plaques adorn the facade of many a building, commemorating noteworthy occupants. Why not pink plaques, for lesbian and gay celebrities?
This is a delightful compendium of gay history with 100 famous lesbians and gays. Includes: Renee Vivien, who wrote over twenty volumes of poetry and prose. Her celebration of lesbian passion and mysticism, and her condemnation of male injustice to women, contributed to her lack of literary recognition; Gertrude Stein, a prolific writer of fiction, verse, drama and criticism. Gertrude's reputation as a literary innovator grew during the 1920s and 30s, she was on her way to becoming one of the most publicised but least read authors of this century; Nancy Spain, journalist, novelist and most famously, a television personality, on such programmes as Jukebox Jury, Twenty Questions and My Word; and Eleanor Rathbone, a vigorous feminist, member of parliament and the moving spirit for family allowances.
ISBN 0-85449-026-4 £6.95

from ALYSON PUBLICATIONS, USA. (distributed in the UK by GMP)

Nancy Toder
CHOICES

Lesbian love can bring joy and passion; it can also bring conflicts. In this straightforward, sensitive novel, Toder conveys the fear and confusion of a woman coming to terms with her sexual and emotional attraction to other women.

'Choices is a classic lesbian love story. It has everything required for a good read: plot, characters, action, erotica. I suspect that it may be the most popular novel since Rubyfruit Jungle.' - Off Our Backs
ISBN 0-932870-619 £5.95

Dell Richards
LESBIAN LISTS

List after list of clever and enlightening trivia for and about lesbians. Columnist Dell Richards has scoured far and wide for this collection of fun facts that will amuse and astonish: banned lesbian books; herbal aphrodisiacs; lesbian ministers and nuns past and present; actresses who've played lesbian characters; lesbian rulers and aristocrats. This is a book you won't be able to put down.
ISBN 1-55583-163-X £6.95

Sarah Holmes, ed
TESTIMONIES: A collection of lesbian coming out stories

Twenty-two women of widely varying backgrounds and ages give accounts of their excitement, passion and conflicts on the journey towards self-discovery.
ISBN 1-55583-121-4 £4.95

Carol S Becker
UNBROKEN TIES

'An important addition to the lesbian literature and community. Becker presents a fascinating account of the diverse experiences of lesbians as they break up, rebuild their lives, and develop varied relationships with ex-lovers. Every lesbian can profit from reading this book.' - JoAnn Loulan, author of Lesbian Passion: Loving Ourselves and Each Other
ISBN 1-55583-106-0 £5.95

GMP/Alyson books can be ordered from any bookshop in the UK, and from specialised bookshops overseas. If you prefer to order by mail, please send full retail price plus £1.50 for postage and packing to: GMP Publishers Ltd (BL), P O Box 247, London N17 9QR.(For Access/Visa/American Express give number and signature.)

In North America order from Alyson Publications Inc, 40 Plympton St, Boston MA 02118, USA.

Name and Address in block letters please:

Name   _____

Address   _____

_____